Vivid experiences of a family's transition from living under a communist dictatorship to a new life in a democratic country, from Cuba to the United States, where this family found freedom.

Living in Freedom!

Teaching and Volunteering, Great Life Experiences

Living in Freedom!

Teaching and Volunteering, Great Life Experiences

Nery Barnet Kircher

Halo
PUBLISHING
INTERNATIONAL

Halo
PUBLISHING
INTERNATIONAL

Halo Publishing International
7550 WIH-10 #800, PMB 2069,
San Antonio, TX 78229

First Edition, April 2024
ISBN: 978-1-63765-583-2
Library of Congress Control Number: 2024904657

The information contained within this book is strictly for informational purposes. Unless otherwise indicated, all the names, characters, businesses, places, events and incidents in this book are either the product of the author's imagination or used in a fictitious manner. Any resemblance to actual persons, living or dead, or actual events is purely coincidental.

Halo Publishing International is a self-publishing company that publishes adult fiction and non-fiction, children's literature, self-help, spiritual, and faith-based books. We continually strive to help authors reach their publishing goals and provide many different services that help them do so. We do not publish books that are deemed to be politically, religiously, or socially disrespectful, or books that are sexually provocative, including erotica. Halo reserves the right to refuse publication of any manuscript if it is deemed not to be in line with our principles. Do you have a book idea you would like us to consider publishing? Please visit www.halopublishing.com for more information.

This book is dedicated to all of those who are seeking freedom or looking for economic opportunities in this great nation, the United States of America.

It takes a lot of adjusting on your part to be able to assimilate and accept this new culture: its language, customs, laws, etc.

Remember, you have been given the opportunity in this new land to find the liberty and chances that were denied in your own country.

Embrace it, respect it, and assimilate into it because not too many countries do something like this for the immigrants and political refugees who come into their land!

May God bless the United States of America!

CONTENTS

Chapter 1

LEAVING COMMUNIST CUBA

As I sat here in my office, in front of my computer, I decided to write my family's memoirs. Let's go back to the years we lived in Cuba. The family nucleus there consisted of my father, my mother, and their five daughters: Marita, Nery (me), Margarita, Julita, and Mirtica. We, the first three ones, were born and grew up in a neighborhood called La Playa, in the city of Matanzas, just two short blocks from the beach.

My mother used to take us to the beach, at 10:00 a.m., together with her sister-in-law Herminia, who lived next door with her three sons, Chito, Tatoño, and Alberto. We are almost the same age because our parents had a double wedding in the chapel at St. Vincent de Paul, my mother's Catholic school. All of us—we three girls, the three boys, and our mothers—enjoyed the no-school summer days at the beach while our fathers were working. This ended ten years later when we moved to the downtown area of the city of Matanzas, away from the beach, closer to my father's job. My younger sisters, Julita and Mirtica, were not able to enjoy the beach as we did.

We Cubans are family oriented and always make it a priority to reach out to our extended family members. We are a big family, and my grandparents were its nucleus. Everyone knows that other family members are there for them in all aspects of their lives. That was the way we grew up in both Cuba and here.

My mother, Maria—we called her Mima—was a piano teacher, and we grew up with an upright piano in our home and listening to my mother playing it. She played children's songs, and we all sang along. We also tried to play the piano that she wanted us so badly to learn, but the only ones who showed an interest were my younger sister Mirtica and I. I did four years of piano lessons at the Condon Ruiz de la Torre Academy when we moved to the center of the city but did not finish. Mirtica tried taking lessons as an adult in Miami, but the teacher advised her to continue playing by ear because her talent was a natural one. She can listen to a song and play it on the piano instantly! We are very happy that one of her great-grandchildren—Margarita's grandson, Frankie Gonzalez, Jr.—is becoming a concert pianist. Best wishes to him in his future career!

Going back to my childhood, I remember seeing my aunts and Grandmother Zoila, sitting around their Philco floor radio and making beautiful tablecloths, bedspreads, etc. while listening to some soap opera. Our paternal aunts, Irma and Mirta, were taught to sew, embroider, and crochet by their mother, Zoila Verrier, and their grandmother,

Maria Barnet. They decorated their house with the things they made. Crocheting was the style then, but they also embroidered.

Upon relocating to the city of Matanzas, we moved into a Spanish-style rowhouse that was more than one hundred years old. It had big brown doors facing a large balcony, and we occupied its second floor, which had a formal living room, family room, three bedrooms, dining room, kitchen, and one-and-a-half bathrooms, plus an interior patio. We always left the doors open so the breeze could run through the house, especially in summer, but insects got in too. When Marita got married six years before our emigration, and a year later had a daughter, Maria Elena, the two bedrooms and terrace on the third floor were assigned to her family.

The first floor was occupied by a family of four sisters and a brother, all single. Four of them passed away while we lived there, and we helped the surviving siblings during these sorrowful times. The last sister, who was left living there alone, was evicted by the Cuban Communist government because they said the house was too big for one person. She was offered two options: go to a nursing home or find a family member who had room for her. She went to live with a niece until her death. In her place, the government moved in a family of fourteen.

In 1961, my father began planning our escape from this regime, so he wanted us to learn English. Marita, Margarita, and I received visas to leave the country through the Peter Pan program. The Peter Pan program began in 1960, and it was organized by the Catholic Church in Miami. More than 14,000 unaccompanied children left Cuba and moved to the USA. In 1962, after Fidel Castro imposed the Iron Curtain during the October missile crisis, nobody was allowed to leave the country; therefore, the program ended. So Marita, Margarita, and I were forced to stay in Cuba. In a way, we were happy because we did not like the idea of going alone to an unknown country and being away from our family.

During this time, my father paid a tutor to teach us English. He wanted us to be ready for our future in the United States of America. As I continued studying, I received teaching and accounting degrees in Cuba. I got both degrees because during the day I went to the school for teachers, and at night I went to the commerce school with my oldest sister, Marita. She received an accounting degree too. The school system then was that when you finished eighth grade—not the twelfth as it is in the USA—you studied the career you wanted, such as teaching, accounting, or arts, or you attended what was called "the Institute" if you desired a more specialized career in medicine, engineering, etc.

As soon as I graduated, I began working in the accounting department at the local polyclinic. Some people came to work wearing their olive-green uniforms to show everyone how loyal to the government they were. I disliked it so much, but there was nothing I could do. That was the way my manager dressed.

I oversaw the petty cash. One day, we had an inspection; the inspector checked my petty cash, and he noticed that ten dollars was missing. Since he knew my family very well, he let me go home to get the money and bring it back. He asked me who else had the key to the petty cash. When I told him that the manager did, the inspector told me that this person was trying to frame me; he advised me to get another job and told me where I could find one.

With the inspector's recommendation, I got a job in the statistics department of the local health system's office. Through my hands passed all the death certificates of those who were sent to the firing squad by the government. Their death certificates read, "Death caused by loss of blood." They were killed because they were considered enemies of the Communist regime, which had taken over the country. I was a young teenager who was very aware of this insanity. Killing those who opposed them? It was too sad for me to see all those young people killed without even a trial!

My father was a partner in a clothing store that was confiscated by the Cuban government. He had to continue working there with a minimum salary, training those who did not know anything about the business. Among them was our cleaning lady, who was made the manager! Marita was working at the store too, but later, when she graduated

from the commerce school, the government sent her to work in the accounting department of the warehouse where all the stores' merchandise was sent before its redistribution to all the expropriated stores. This was a new system created by the Communist regime. Marita met her future husband, Rolando, at the warehouse; he also worked there.

In 1965, my parents decided to begin the necessary paperwork, so all of us could leave the country together, since the Peter Pan program where we were living had ended. The rest of the family applied for USA visas too! As soon as those documents were presented to the Cuban government, we could no longer work, so we all needed to do something right away to bring money into the household. Two of my sisters, Marita and Julita, began knitting baby clothes, sweaters, and other items, and I began crocheting pantyhose and socks for ladies and men. My aunts, Irma and Mirta, taught me how to make them since, before that, I had no idea how to crochet. They also taught Julita to knit. When we came to the USA, my father was wearing the socks I made for him, and I brought one pair of pantyhose for each of the ladies traveling with us. Marita learned how to knit from some old family friends whom she then helped fill their many orders for handmade products.

One of my father's friends asked him if he could help install television antennas, for which he would be paid. With this money, we were able to cover the house expenses and buy groceries, which were rationed at this point by the government. Still today, in 2024, after sixty-five years of Communist dictatorship, each household is assigned a quota for purchasing merchandise, including not only food but also clothing, toys, and everything needed in your life; everything is controlled by the government. Unbelievable!

Marita and Rolando got married in 1965. Her husband continued working since the government did not consider him part of our family's nucleus. They were not married when the visa documents were presented to the government. Marita was able to add her daughter at birth and her husband later. Rolando paid for their household expenses, and Marita gave our family a helping hand by knitting.

The teaching profession has run in our family for several generations. From school administrators, principals, teachers, and even a janitor. Yes, janitor! Later, when we moved to a neighborhood south of Miami, my father, Antonio, whom we called Pipo, was offered a job as a school janitor, and he took it. He was already fifty-six years old, so he thought about the benefits of this public-school job. He was right! When he retired from the school system at the age of sixty-six, he received not only his social security check, but a pension too. After retiring, he continued working at the gas station that belonged to my husband's family.

The Communist government wanted teachers who could teach their students the Communist doctrine. Special schools were created to educate and train these new teachers. The old schools for teachers were closed, and all the students were transferred to a school in Havana called Makarenko to foster the new Socialist/Communist mentality. They needed all the teachers to learn how to teach the new curriculum geared toward Karl Marx's and Lenin's teachings. My friends and I, who were ideologically opposed to the Communist point of view, were not permitted to teach in Cuba!

Even though I was not allowed to work, one of the neighbors asked me if I could tutor her son, a cute eight-year-old. This neighbor really wanted to help us too. I agreed to teach him and began doing so right away, twice a week. He was having problems with his math. During his lessons, we sat at the dining room table. One day, I noticed that he was not paying attention to me; it was as if his mind were somewhere else.

I asked him what happened to him, but his answer was, "Nothing." So I continued with the lesson. Again, I noticed that he was distracted, and both of his hands were under the table. I dropped my pencil on the floor so I could see where his hands were when I picked it up. To my disbelief, he was playing with himself. Immediately, I asked him to place both hands on the table. I needed him to stop this behavior! No wonder he was having trouble at school! He could not concentrate while he was playing with himself!

Well, things began to get better because from that day on, I always made sure his arms were on the table, ready to use his pencil. I did not mention it to his mother since I did not want her to stop my lessons. We needed the money! I prayed for this child not to have any more problems later in life. By the end of the year, this family had left the country, and I have never heard from them again.

I also taught French to a student who was attending the language school the government created. At the time, Russian, instead of English, was the language taught in schools as a second language. I really did not want to teach this lady since she was working at one of the government's offices, and she wore the Communist military uniform. I was afraid she was coming to spy on us, but she insisted I teach her, and I was afraid to say no. She came at night twice a week so we could go over the learned lessons at her school and practice some French conversation. Thank God she came wearing civilian clothes, not the olive-green uniform I always saw her wearing.

At that time, I had already graduated from the L'Alliance Francaise school in Havana with a French degree. My dear friend Estela and I took a bus to Havana every Saturday to attend this school. It took me five years of French to receive this degree. Nobody else in my immediate family spoke French, and my sisters used to get mad at me when I practiced talking to them in French. I just laughed!

Things were getting more difficult every day. We were watched by many of our so-called friends who had become informants of the Communist regime to win trust and be given better opportunities within the government. We could not trust anyone! Parents could not trust their own children and vice versa. It was a very scary situation, always looking over your shoulder before speaking, and communicating very carefully so your words would not be taken the wrong way, which could create a bigger problem for you with the Communist leaders.

In April 1968, my sister Margarita was able to leave for Mexico. I was supposed to leave with her, but the Mexican consulate denied my visa. It was a very sad time for us. She did not want to leave, but my parents told her she must so that she could help the rest of us get out of that hell. While in Mexico, Margarita was able to send us the material we needed to continue making and selling the socks, hosiery, etc. to bring in some money. We were happy because she did not have to endure the forced-labor camps as my father and I had.

It is understandable that boys who were of military age, fifteen to twenty-seven, were not allowed to leave the country. They had to continue living in that hellhole. Even though they did not like that totalitarian system, they had to be hypocrites and show a different face at school, work, or anywhere they wanted to be accepted; otherwise, they would be in the same situation we were. For these young boys to continue attending school to receive a higher education, they had to become the new Marxist-Leninist man, had to belong to the Communist Youth, and later had to join the Communist party while in college. This was and still is a hypocritical situation. It must have been hard for many of them to live like that.

The Communist government concentrated on the creation of the new Socialist/Communist man. The young were indoctrinated in school, and workers were forced to do volunteer work at their jobs; otherwise, they could be considered undesirable citizens. People stopped attending churches because the Communist belief system was atheistic. You were not supposed to worship God, but the new Communist leader, Fidel Castro. If there was a demonstration, you were forced to attend so you avoided reprisals from managers, coworkers, and the Communist regime.

Many were leaving the country, and this was making Fidel Castro angry. He created forced-labor camps, so those who wished to leave the country had to pay their way out. At the beginning of June 1968, my father and I received a letter from the government ordering us to report on June 21 to an area where many buses were waiting to take us to an undisclosed place. Women were separated from men. My mother was desperate; she did not know where we were taken or what was going to happen to us. Our parents were glad that Margarita was able to leave the country in April and was in Mexico.

The feeling of going to the unknown was overwhelming for all the women who were riding with me on the bus. Leaving behind our families and not knowing where they were taking us, what kind of punishment we were going to receive, and many more questions caused us frustration and desperation. Apparently, this camp was far away from home, as we were riding for hours.

When we got there, we passed a double-wire fence guarded by the militia. When we got off the buses, we had to form several lines in front of all these encampments where we were going to sleep. We were about 300 women! Each of us was assigned a number that we were going to be called by every morning. Soldiers were the ones giving us all these instructions. What was this? A forced-labor camp or a jail?

In the morning, we were awakened by a loud noise and told to get ready to work in the fields. When we were all outside the barracks, we were told to go to the dining area for breakfast. It consisted of coffee made of *chicharos* (split peas) and some *gofio* (wheat flour) that we put into the coffee.

We were all worried about how long the government was going to keep us there and what kind of work we were going to do. Were we going to be allowed to leave the country to go to the USA? Young and old women faced the uncertainty of a shaky future. Could we trust each other? Why were soldiers guarding the camp?

My stomach was in knots, and I was worried about what kind of circumstances were ahead of us. I could not keep anything down; I threw up whatever I ate and had nonstop diarrhea. My weight dropped dramatically. I did not have too many friends in the camp since most of them already had left the country. Some with Spanish families went back to Spain and others to the United States. We were sent to these forced-labor camps as a punishment for wanting to leave the country!

The camp I was taken to was on a farm called Cejas 2 in Pedro Betancourt, a town in the province of Matanzas. At the beginning, we were allowed to go home once a month, but when it got more difficult for the government to feed 300 women and to provide for their monthly needs, we were allowed to go home every two weeks. The camp was guarded by armed soldiers as if we were in prison! I continued crocheting at the camp in the evenings, something that helped me keep my mind off my current situation. Besides that, we needed the money more than ever. When the Friday came that we were allowed to leave, we had to find our own way back home! Imagine all of us out in the road trying

to find someone to take us home, which was about three hours away.

My father was sent to a camp far away from home and was allowed to come home after six months. He had to have hand surgery to fix the tendon he injured while cutting sugar cane. He was then transferred to a camp closer to home and was able to come home every month until our departure. My mother was not sent to these forced-labor camps because she was taking care of my two younger sisters, Julita and Mirtica. Marita was taking care of her toddler daughter, so she was allowed to stay home too.

I began feeling depressed and sick at the camp. After almost a year, one weekend I asked permission to go to the doctor on Monday. I had several tests done, and the doctor found that I was suffering from hypothyroidism. Due to this health issue, I was transferred to a camp not too far from home, so I was able to sleep in my own bed again. It was a little bit of brightness in a dark sky.

At this new camp, our brigade was under the supervision of a soldier named Manuel. Every day, he threatened that if we did something wrong to the plants, it would be considered sabotaging the country's production. When we were working in the *malanga* fields, he threatened to check our *mochilas* (backpacks) at the end of the day to make sure we were not taking anything home. The ironic thing was that, many times at the end of a hardworking day, on the way home, the truck stopped in front of the home of someone who was a high-ranking military officer, and Manuel dropped off a sack of malanga.

My father and I spent three years doing hard work at different camps until the moment we were allowed to leave the country. Because of the visa process, Fidel Castro's Communist government knew who wanted to leave the country, and they assumed this was because they disliked the revolution and disagreed with the new regime. You were marked as an undesirable, a counterrevolutionary, a worm, and many more degrading words. You were persecuted and constantly harassed and watched by the gestapo. It was not an easy time in our lives. I wrote all about this time in my book *Path to Freedom* (also in Spanish, *Camino a la Libertad*).

This is the last family picture we had taken in Cuba. It was on Mother's Day in May 1971, a month before we were allowed to leave the country. Margarita is missing from the picture because she was already living in Mexico.

Several of our family members distanced themselves from us

because they did not want to be marked as counterrevolutionaries, as we were. They could not even be in touch with family members who had already left the country and were living in the USA or other countries. People feared reprisals and losing their identification with the new system that Fidel Castro was imposing on the population.

On June 19, 1971, when we were in the truck coming back from the fields, the driver took a different route and dropped me right in front of my house. As soon as I got there, I saw my family outside in the street. The government had sent an official to the house; he checked the inventory of everything in the house, which the soldiers had taken when my father presented the required documentation to leave the country. After they checked that all the furniture and articles, including my father's car, which were listed in the inventory were there and in good working condition, the government official told my mother to get only one change of clothing for each of us, including my father's and mine, as we were not yet home. This soldier put a seal on the front door, so neither we nor anyone else could go back inside. All our mementos, clothing, and other things that meant something to us were left behind in what we called home!

Our mother's uncle, Secundino, lived in the corner house, so we went there. I was able to take a shower and put on some clean clothes. My father arrived the next day to find a seal on the front door and his car still in the *zaguán*, the downstairs foyer where he kept it. That morning, my uncle took me back to the camp to return the boots the government had given me.

In the afternoon, we went to the airport. We spent the night there since we had to wait hours for the plane to come first thing in the morning. When we presented our passports, they took them and stamped them with the word *null*. They did not return them to us. Thank God my mother had an envelope with important documents, including our birth certificates, in her purse.

On June 22, we were allowed to leave Cuba on the Freedom Flights. These flights were created and supported by the US government after the forced closing of the Camarioca Exodus, a port between the city of Matanzas and Varadero. This happened when, in September 1965, Fidel Castro announced that anyone who had relatives in the United States and wanted to leave the island could do so. They had to come by boat to pick up their relatives at the Camarioca port. We were claimed by some relatives who lived in Miami. But because of the weather, this exodus stopped within a few months, and those families who were still waiting to leave were allowed to do so on the Freedom Flights created by the US government. These flights continued until 1973.

When we boarded the plane, we were anxious. It was our first time flying! Still, we were afraid that anything could happen, and we would be forced to go back to Cuba, as had happened to some of our teenage friends, Maria and

Raul, during the Peter Pan program. They were in the plane when Fidel Castro imposed the Iron Curtain and stopped all the flights; therefore, they were ordered to deplane.

As soon as our plane lifted into the sky, and we could see the island under us, the pilot said, "Welcome to the USA!"

We felt finally free from that dictatorship! We all began singing the Cuban national anthem with tears falling down our cheeks. The feeling of freedom was indescribable! It was such an emotional moment that we will never forget. Leaving behind close family members was hard, but we knew we would help them leave Cuba later. It was also very hard to leave our thirteen-year-old, spoiled dog. She always slept with us. We were lucky that one of the neighbors kept her, but unfortunately this neighbor died a year later of brain cancer. Her husband got rid of the dog by taking it to a camp where she died a few years after. We hope that at least our dear dog was not hungry, but for sure, at the time of her death, she missed the warmth of our bodies, the pampering, and the love that we all gave her. When we heard the news, it really broke our hearts, thinking of her and the way she lived the last years of her life.

Chapter 2

REMEMBERING MY ANCESTORS

There are two important things about my ancestors I learned after publishing my book *Path to Freedom*, which tells the story of their arrival in Cuba and life there before and after Fidel Castro, until our emigration to the USA. First, on my father's Barnet side, my sister Mirtica found out, looking at England's marriage records, that in 1829, Maria Barnet married William Drake, who we believe is a descendant of Sir Francis Drake's family. What a coincidence—our great-grandmother's name was also Maria Nestora Barnet and Roque de Escobar. She was born in Barcelona, Spain.

This is my great-grandmother when she was a very young woman. She had beautiful blue eyes and brown hair. She married Eusebio Luis Verrier and

Gabaud from Nantes, France. I remember her when she was in her seventies; she died in her eighties.

According to Wikipedia, Edmund Drake, a Protestant farmer, and his wife, Mary Mylwaye, had twelve sons. The Drakes were related to the Hawkins family of Plymouth, who were shipowners, merchants, and privateers. Their oldest son, Sir Francis Drake, was the first Englishman to attempt the circumnavigation of the globe and the second ever to complete it. These efforts were fronts for a secret pirate mission sanctioned by Queen Elizabeth I against the Spanish. Sir Francis Drake is also known for making several voyages to the West Indies as a slave trader. He also served as the mayor of Plymouth in England. During his global travels, he explored much of the northwestern part of the modern United States. His strong dislike for the Spanish motivated him to destroy and loot as many Spanish vessels as possible. Some would call Sir Francis Drake a pirate; others would call him a privateer.

Who was going to tell us that we are descendants of the Drake family! It was very interesting to learn about this part of my father's family. We have not found out for sure yet if our Barnet ancestors were from England or Scotland and why they left for Barcelona, Spain, and from there to Matanzas, Cuba.

I am writing this so future generations have an idea who their ancestors were. Besides that, writing has brought something new to my life during my retirement, especially during the COVID epidemic when I was able to finish and publish three books: *Path to Freedom, Camino a la Libertad, and A Diary of My Dying Father*. It was really an enjoyable time writing them and then seeing the final product. My dear husband, Bob, and our sons Bobby and Marc always encouraged me to write down all the stories I told them about our life in Cuba.

Above, a beautiful picture of our French side of the family, the Verriers, in 1921. As soon as Great-grandmother Maria met the French man who would become Great-grandfather Eusebio, the tall man in the back row, she fell in love. He was a handsome man who would do anything for her. They had eight children—four girls and four boys.

Their two older sons are not in the picture. Great-grand-mother Maria is standing in front of Great-grandfather, and Grandmother Zoila is to the right of her. Grandfather Antonio Barnet is on the right, holding our father; he was only a few months old when this picture was taken. Grandfather Barnet is sitting in front of my grandmother. Great-aunt Silvia Verrier was a very well-known teacher in the city of Matanzas. She is the young lady sitting on the left. She inherited her father's green eyes. She was very intelligent, well educated, and a six-foot-tall woman. She came to visit my parents in the USA when she was ninety. She did her best to speak to Bob in English, but was surprised when he answered her in Spanish. My great-grandparents also had many grandchildren.

This is a nice picture of Grandmother Zoila Verrier together with Grandfather Antonio Barnet and my father. We called them *Abuela* (Grandmother) and *Abuelo* (Grandfather). Abuela had beautiful, big brown eyes, and Abuelo had nice green eyes. They had four children: my father—Antonio, Jr.—then Irma, Mirta, and Gonzalo. The boys had beautiful green eyes and the girls the most beautiful dark-blue eyes I have seen. Abuela died at fifty years of age, too young, and Abuelo passed away when he was seventy-six. All their children emigrated to the USA with their families. They were able to provide for their children a life of freedom in this, our great nation. They all became American citizens.

Now I need to tell you something about my mother's Martinez side of the family. My cousin Chito's daughter, Lizbet, was searching for our ancestors, and she found some information that dates back to the Cuban war for independence from Spain in 1896. My great-grandparents—Antonio Martínez y Ojeda, who was born in Las Palmas de Gran Canaria, in the Canary Islands, and his wife, Francisca Suárez y Suárez, who was born in Cuba, but her parents were from the Canary Islands too—were able to depart on a ship with their nine children while my great-grandmother was pregnant with my Grandmother Aurora. At the time, life in Cuba was getting too dangerous for Spaniards.

A few days before their departure, soldiers came looking for Antonio. Francisca opened the door, a rifle in hand; they always hid it under the bed. She answered the door and told them that her husband was not at home, that he went to town. Antonio was hiding under the bed! The soldiers told her they would come back for him. The Spanish soldiers then went to Antonio's parents' home. His father, Mateo Martinez, and his mother experienced something horrible.

What the Spanish soldiers were doing to the Cuban population at the time is recorded in a US congressional document from 1896. One of the documented cases recounts what happened to our Martinez great-great-grandparents. The Cuban guerrillas stopped at the home of Antonio's parents on the way to Calimete in the province of Matanzas. Days before, my great-great-grandfather, Mateo Martinez, was forced to enlist in a body of insurgents under the command of Juan Pablo Jabio while their troop was staying at his farm. He then heard that the Spanish soldiers were coming to his house, looking for him. He decided to run into the forest. His wife told him that she wished to stay at home because she was sure she would be fine.

The Spaniards stopped at their house, and the officer inquired as to the whereabouts of her husband, Mateo Martinez, pictured above.

"Indeed, I can't tell you," she replied.

"I'll make you," said the Spanish soldier, and he proceeded to tear off her clothing and rape her. He then questioned her anew. Receiving no answer from her because she was crying hysterically at this point, he unsheathed his sword and resorted to cutting and slashing his victim until her blood covered the floor and she lay unconscious in a corner. Her shrieks and entreaties only served to encourage brutal laughter from the soldiers.

Incidents like these inflamed anti-Spanish sentiments during the Spanish-American war in Cuba.

When Mateo came back home the next day and saw what happened to his wife, he could not believe what the Spanish soldier had done to her. His adult children came, and she was buried. The next day, they were able to get away and board a ship named *Covadonga*, headed for Spain, with the rest of the family. The trip took months to get to the Canary Islands. During the trip, some people came down with bad cases of chicken pox. The sickness spread throughout the ship and killed many. The bodies of the deceased were thrown overboard to avoid the spread of the sickness. Antonio and his wife lost their eleven-year-old daughter, Margarita, and two more children, ages nine and six, during this trip. Since they were getting close to Tenerife, another of the Canary Islands, they begged the officers to please let them keep their children so they could bury them as soon as they touched land, which could be seen in the distance. They buried their three children in Tenerife then continued to San Bartolome de Tirajana in Las Palmas, where they were from and had relatives. Francisca later gave birth to Aurora, my grandmother, and two more children.

My sister Mirtica, while looking at official records from the Canary Islands, found that my great-grandfather, Antonio Martinez, then thirty-eight years old, bought six farms, according to Spanish real estate documents from those years. We believe that these farms were bought to accommodate the entire family, all of whom were able to leave Cuba.

My great-great-grandfather, Mateo Martinez, never went back to Cuba. He could not confront again the place or the awful memory of how he found his wife assassinated there. His son, Antonio, my great-grandfather, went back to Cuba and bought a forty-hectare farm, which they called *Finca El Sol*. This farm was located by the Canimar River and had some beachfront property on the Matanzas bay. Next to their farm was the very well-known Cabarrocas farm. These are beautiful places on the coast of Matanzas. Prior to Castro's dictatorship, the Cuban government had to obtain the Martinez family's permission to build the beautiful Canimar Bridge that takes you to Varadero Beach.

Great-grandmother Francisca had a total of twenty children. Grandmother Aurora always spoke of how beautiful the farm was, and everything reminded her of the great time she had growing up there. Unfortunately, one of my great-grandmother's children drowned in the Canimar River at twenty-two years of age. They were hardworking farmers who had to endure death, running for freedom, living in exile, and returning to their roots. Unfortunately, their next generation had to suffer similar circumstances in the name of "freedom" when they had to emigrate to the United States of America.

Chapter 3

BEGINNING A NEW LIFE
IN FREEDOM

Even though years have passed, there are some things that are still vivid in my mind, such as arriving in a new country with nothing, building a new life, teaching, and volunteering. In moving to the USA, some of our experiences were good, some were not that good, and some were funny. I am aware that others had horrible experiences, but in our case, they were not as traumatic as some of the stories we have heard from other immigrants. Now, as we look back, my husband and I laugh about them! Time is passing so fast that before my life is gone, I want others to know what it meant for us to begin a new life in another country with a different language and culture.

After arriving in the United States of America in 1971, we spent a few days in Miami. Some of our friends who had arrived a few years before us came to see us at the Freedom Tower. One of them, Felito, took us around the city and to a shoe store after he heard my younger sister Mirtica complaining that her feet were hurting because her shoes were too small. He bought her a new pair of shoes. His parents also invited us for dinner at their house that night. What a delicious dinner and enjoyable evening we all had!

The next day, we flew up north to Boston, Massachusetts, and from there, to a small town a few hours away, Worcester, where my sister Margarita; her husband, Frank; Grandmother Aurora; my mother's sister, Aunt Marta; and her son, Mayito, lived. All the members of our family who were in exile and living up north in nearby cities came to welcome us at the Boston airport. Among them, Aunt Irma with her husband Julio and her children, Zoila and Julio Antonio; Cousin Chito, whose wife Magaly and their children were still in Spain. It was a very emotional moment!

Our mother was very happy to be reunited with her mother and Margarita; Pipo was also thrilled to be among my mother's closest family members. We were all happy because we were finally breathing the air of freedom!

People who arrive here from Cuba think that the ones who came before them have the money to help the ones who just arrived or are visiting from Cuba, or even the money to help their family in Cuba. The reality is that you must work very hard to pay for the essential things of life, and there is not much money left after paying all your monthly debts. It takes some years to become better established so you can enjoy vacations, purchase things needed at home, and help others. We were aware of this before we arrived because our family had told us. Thank God we were able to work with the green card the government gave us. We were considered political refugees because we departed from a Communist country where we were persecuted, so that made it easier for us.

Margarita arrived in the United States in 1970 after spending two years in Mexico City. She got married in June 1970, a year before we arrived. We were sorry that we could not be there with her at this important time of her life. She met her husband, Frank, a young Cuban coworker who escaped from Cuba on a tiny boat several years before she did. Aunt Irma, my father's sister, and her family lived in New Jersey, as did my cousin Chito and his family. They all came a few years before we did.

We were very happy to finally be free and with our dear family in the United States of America where we found the freedom we had lost in our own country. Sadly, a week before our arrival, my cousin Mayito was drafted into the US Army. It was very hard to see Mayito leave; we worried that he could be sent to the war in Vietnam, and we were especially concerned about his mother, Aunt Marta.

Thank God he stayed at a base in New Jersey; a year later, he was sent to a base in California. It was both a happy and a sad time for the family.

Our father began working at the same factory at which my brother-in-law Frank was working. Margarita and Marta had become employed there too before we came. Margarita stopped working after she got pregnant, and Aunt Marta left when she received her teaching certification and began working as a teacher in the bilingual school.

Cubans in the neighborhood began calling us the Diamond Sisters because we did not have to go to work at the factory right away, as did most Cubans when they first arrived. Oh, well, we were lucky that my younger sisters enrolled in school, and I got a job in September at the school where my aunt was working while going to college at night. Marita stayed home and took care of Maria Elena until she began school after she reached the age of five that September.

Maria Elena cried and cried because she did not understand her teacher and the kids in the classroom. She was very scared, and it was very traumatic for her. We tried to get her to attend the bilingual school at which my aunt and I were working, but it was not possible. After a while, she met other Spanish-speaking classmates and was able to adjust to the school.

For Cuban refugees, it is imperative that their children learn the English language, receive an education, and become a part of the melting pot. Still, we kept our customs and spoke our language at home. All our children speak Spanish, too, because my mother spoke to them only in Spanish to make sure they did not forget their roots. My kids were the ones whose Spanish was not that great. As children, when I spoke to them in Spanish, many times I was told they hated it. I stopped using it and left it up to them. Today, Bobby is more fluent than Marc, but both can understand and communicate in Spanish.

Mima began working at a sewing factory, and with the money she made, she put a down payment on a new upright piano, which she paid off weekly, little by little. We enjoyed listening to her playing the piano again. Mirtica and I played it too. After a while, my father asked my mother to stay home so she could be a housewife again since we were all working and making enough to support our home.

One Sunday, my father invited a friend to visit our home. He was a young Colombian engineer who worked with him in the factory. He wanted me to play the piano for them. They sat in two armchairs we had next to the piano and smoked cigarettes while listening to the music.

At one point, I looked at my father's friend and saw smoke coming from the side of the chair in which he was sitting. I thought, *Is it from the cigarette?* Then I looked again and noticed that his chair was actually on fire.

My father ran to the kitchen and came back with a pail of water. He put out the fire, but the chair was ruined. That was the end of this special moment for them. After the friend left, we laughed about it, but my mom was upset about the chair.

The government gave my father a small stipend when we arrived. As soon as my father began working at one of the local factories, he informed the social worker that, thank God, we did not need help anymore, that we had jobs to support ourselves. He was a very hardworking man and hated handouts.

Right after our arrival, we found an apartment next to the building where my sister Margarita lived, and Marita found an apartment for her family in Margarita's building. Grandmother Aurora and Aunt Marta lived in the building on the corner, across the street. My grandmother was glad we all were able to find a home in the same city. These were tall, old brown-brick buildings near Clark University. We were all together in the same block of Lincoln Street. Marita's husband, Roly, came six months after our arrival, and we were able to celebrate all together our first Christmas in freedom. He also began working at the factory.

Our apartment was a nice size. It had a living room with a window to the street, next to it a small room where my mother had her piano; that room also had a window to the street . Down the hall, three bedrooms and only one bathroom, a dining-kitchen area, and a pantry. At the back of the building, we had a balcony with stairs to the ground floor. We asked the owner, Mr. Forsley, to leave the old furniture, which had been abandoned by the previous tenant. He even let us use other furniture he had stored in the basement. My parents were in the first bedroom, Julita and Mirtica in the second one, and I was in a tiny bedroom next to the kitchen; it was just large enough for a twin bed, a dresser with a mirror, and a nightstand. My parents purchased a colonial-style living room set, a queen bed, and two twin beds for my sisters. Friends also gave us some old furniture that completed the décor.

I must let you know our first impression of the nearby shopping center. Most of the businesses were run by Americans, and because the employees acted as if they did not understand my English, it was sometimes difficult to communicate. I had a feeling that when they heard my accent, they just acted as if they could not understand me.

We could not believe all the food for cats and dogs! The first time we saw it, we thought it was for human consumption. Margarita showed us what to get since it was very confusing to go through all those lines full of food. We could not believe that all of that was there for us to purchase. Several times, we had to put back some things because we did not have enough money, especially for things that we really did not need. The feeling was overwhelming, especially after years of being told exactly what we were allowed to buy and finding that in short supply in Cuba.

When we went to a clothing store for the first time, we were surprised to find so many nice things we had not seen since the Communist regime had taken over in Cuba. The clothing stores were beautiful in the US, as they had been in Cuba before the revolution, and we spent time looking at things just out of curiosity, especially my father who knew about this type of merchandise. I realize that the security guard was keeping an eye on us. Of course, we acted as if we were children in a toy store! We could not believe all that merchandise. It was amazing! It took us a while to get used to seeing so much. In Cuba, everything was rationed, and still today, after sixty-five years, you can only purchase what the government allows you. The difference between Cuba and the US was a real culture shock!

Aunt Marta took us to a secondhand store where my father bought a nice portable radio with several bands, so he listened to Cuba's news occasionally and the *Voice of the America* programs, as he used to do in Cuba. I purchased a small record player and bought some old records they had for sale. My mother bought a nice set of glasses and other things she needed in the kitchen. We purchased even clothes, especially for my father. Their prices were unbelievable in comparison with the stores we visited, and everything still looked new.

We arrived in June, and the weather was welcoming. It was the 1970s, the hippies era, and we were all surprised to see how the youth were dressed: the miniskirts, go-go boots, tights, bodysuits, and bell-bottoms; the lack of bras; women with flowers in their long hair; men with long hair; and Afros too. Other cultural shocks we all received!

We met some students from South America while attending night school at a nearby college. They took us to parks, picnics, bowling alleys, skating rinks, etc. We also went to baseball games with Margarita and her husband, Frank. Every weekend, we went bowling, and it was there that Julita met her future husband, Milton, who was from Ecuador. He was ten years older than she and divorced with children.

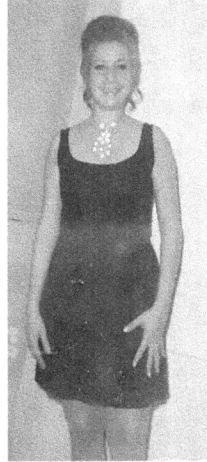

The weather was beautiful, and the days were very long, so we really enjoyed the freedom we had in this new country. I began wearing body shirts with miniskirts and boots too!

We walked through downtown to go to school and church. One Sunday on the way to church, we hitchhiked, and a guy gave us a ride. When we got to church, Father Smith asked us how we got there. We told him what we did, that someone gave us a ride. He begged us not to do that anymore because it was too dangerous. He found someone from church to pick us up and bring us to Mass.

Another day, we were walking to school when a car slowed down, and the driver began calling to us. As we approached the car, we noticed that this guy was exposing and touching himself. It was very scary, especially after what Father Smith told us. We ran to school as fast as we could!

Aunt Marta, who was a Spanish-language teacher in Cuba, had revalidated her degree by then, and she was already teaching at the bilingual elementary school in the city. She was the first bilingual teacher at this center! She taught third grade to students who spoke only Spanish and were new arrivals in the USA. They were taken away for an hour to another classroom with an English teacher to learn the new language. At the same time, this teacher sent her American students to receive Spanish as a second language in Marta's classroom. At night school, Aunt Marta prepared Spanish-speaking students to receive their high school diplomas. She also taught Spanish at college. I am very proud of my dedicated, hardworking Aunt Marta! She was also lucky to have had her mother helping her by taking care of the household and meals.

Our father's sister, Aunt Irma, who was a school principal in Cuba, was not that lucky. She came over with two very young children, and only some of her husband's relatives were nearby. Her husband began working in a factory while she was doing sewing work for a factory at home. She was not able to go back to school to revalidate her Cuban teaching degree, so her situation was more difficult. Aunt Marta invited her to move to the same city where we were, so she could work in the same bilingual school, but since they did not know how to drive—something that was urgently needed to go to work and school in the USA—she decided to stay in Union City, New Jersey. She never taught again.

Aunt Marta's school was a transitional bilingual school designed to help Spanish-speaking children assimilate into the English regular-school curriculum. Aunt Marta arranged for me to have an interview with the school principal. During this interview, the principal wanted to know how things were in Cuba. I was afraid to talk about my experiences in the forced-labor camps and all the humiliations we had to suffer there. I felt that there were Cuban spies here too, where their tentacles could reach me. I gave him the simple answer, "Bad, I am glad I am here." I was not even aware of the disputes among the different political parties here in US. I simply was afraid of Communists. Aunt Marta reassured me that I could talk to people about my experiences in Cuba, that it was okay, that she understood how I was feeling.

I was given a job as a teacher's assistant and began attending college at night to revalidate my teaching degree.

I began work by assisting the fourth-grade teacher, whom I will call

Teddy. I tutored children who were falling behind in the regular classroom and helped him with many classroom tasks. Teddy, to whom I was assigned to assist, welcomed me with open arms. After a while, he became my first American friend. He was of Polish descent and even took me to dance the polka at the local Polish club one day. I loved it!

Teddy was so surprised that I knew how to dance the polka. I explained to him that when we were going to an all-girls private Catholic school in Cuba, the gym teacher taught us how to dance different folkloric dances as a form of exercise. We learned all types of dances, like the cha-cha, rumba, merengue, *jarabe tapatío*, polka, etc. He also invited me to go with his mother and sister to see the play *Jesus Christ Superstar* in Boston. We had a great time, and I was glad he invited me.

Sometimes Teddy gave me a ride home from work, and I loved that he played all the newest music on the radio. Aunt Marta always tuned into Spanish radio stations and listened to their music. I will never forget some of the American songs that were played on the radio then.

After we moved to Miami, I never heard from Teddy again. We were so busy trying to reorganize our lives that perhaps I neglected to contact him too. Anyways, he was working with my aunt, and he could find out about us from her. Sometime later in life, I called his home. His mother answered, and she told me that Teddy had moved to Boston and that she did not know his phone number.

She was surprised that I had called him after several years. To me, he was my first American friend, and I am very thankful for that.

The children in the class where I was assigned to work were more advanced in English, and the lessons were all taught in that language. I helped those who needed personal assistance. These students were placed in this classroom because they were getting ready to transition into a regular classroom that followed the regular educational curriculum. I was so excited to be able to work at this school even though I was still having some problems with the pronunciation of some English words and with some idiomatic expressions. During lunch, I went to the teachers' lunchroom with my leading teacher. I loved to listen to the teachers conversing about their experiences while I paid attention to what they were saying, how they were saying it, and surely learning. I felt shy about speaking because I was afraid to say something wrong.

One day, Teddy could not go to the lunchroom because he had something to do elsewhere. I decided to go anyways. The other teachers began asking me questions. One of the things I said was that I loved to go to the beach, but with my accent it sounded like "bitch." Those teachers began laughing so hard that it embarrassed me. After that, I was afraid to say anything else and stayed quiet.

Another day that I was by myself again, some of them began asking me questions about my life. In the conversation, we were talking about things in the house, and I mentioned that we were looking for twin sheets, but the way I said "sheet" sounded like "shit." This time, instead of acting embarrassed, I simply began laughing with them, enjoying the moment and not giving them the satisfaction of embarrassing me. I did not let this intimidate me anymore. I said, "You guys know very well what I meant. I would love you to teach me the correct pronunciation instead of laughing." After that, their attitudes changed, and they became friendlier and began helping me to say those words the correct way. No more laughing at me, just colleagues helping another colleague.

It is not easy to communicate when others are waiting for you to mispronounce a word so they can make fun of you. It was degrading, and I am sure many have gone through the same experience I went through. Sometimes people do not realize how cruel they can be when someone is trying so hard to speak another language with sounds that are strange to them. It was a daunting time to start a new life in a different country with a different culture and a different language. It was similar to the beginning of a child's life—learning to crawl, then to walk, and in the end, to run.

Finally, I was able to purchase a used car for $400 with the money I had saved; it was a gold 1965 Ford Galaxie. Wow, my first car in the USA! I already knew how to drive since Grandfather Juan and my father taught me in Cuba. I got my driver's license, and we were so happy that we could now go places, such as to school, to shop, to visit our new friends, and just to enjoy the freedom this new country offered us. We did not have to walk through the downtown area to go to school and church anymore! Julita, Mirtica, and I are pictured with my new car, ready to go for a ride. You can see our building behind us. I still rode with my aunt to work, and my father drove my car sometimes.

When I began college, I was invited to go out by one of my classmates, an American guy. He was surprised when I asked him if I could bring one of my sisters. After that, the invitation was rescinded. The guy explained to me that after dinner, he had planned to take me to his apartment to listen to music and have a more intimate "good time." When I explained to him that I was doing my best to stay away from temptation since I was saving myself for marriage, he could not believe it; he even asked if I was a lesbian or if something was wrong with me.

In November, we met a group of South American students while we were bowling. We began socializing with them. They understood why we were the way we were.

Julita fell in love with one of them, Milton, and they got married in February of the following year.

In December, all these new friends organized a party for my birthday. My mother made a Cuban dinner, and we had typical dishes from the countries of some of the guests who had brought food. Our friends began getting there around 8:00 p.m. Some guests also brought their typical music, like *cumbias*, since most of them were from Colombia and Ecuador. We continued dancing the *cumbia* until about 4:00 a.m. My parents could not believe no one would leave since it was already past midnight! What a great party I had! It was a lot of fun; plus, I received many gifts of things that I needed.

The next day, the apartment was very dirty because the wax on the wood floors had been rubbed off during all the dancing. As soon as we woke up, we had to clean the place and wax the floors again. We did not care since we had enjoyed the party so much. All these youngsters were so nice and clean-cut; we were happy to have met them.

Going back to school, one day, Teddy asked me to pass out pencils to the students. When I got to one of them, Joe, he said, "I don't want this fucking pencil."

I smiled at him and said, "It's okay."

Teddy, who was sitting behind his desk, asked me, "What did Joe say?"

With a smile on my face, I said aloud, "That he does not want this fucking pencil."

All the students began laughing. Teddy jumped over his desk and ran to my side, moved me to a corner, and told me that I said a bad word. I told him I did not know it was a bad word, but I thought it was the brand of the pencil. At that point, the students realized I did not know any of the bad words, and that created a big problem for me in the classroom. They used them with me!

Now, I realize that Joe had some emotional problems. He was always very hyper. One day, we were going outside for recess, and I had all the students in line. Joe was the first one in line so I could take ahold of him. He was desperate to run outside, but I was telling him he had to wait until the bell rang. He suddenly took off, and I was left with his shirt in my hands. I could not believe it! Then the bell rang, and I looked for him to make sure he put his shirt back on, even without some of the buttons.

I was still young and had no experience at all with the facts of life. My father was always on top of us, telling us how we needed to keep our dignity and be good girls. Therefore, we were not allowed to go to parties without chaperones. Thank God there were five sisters, and we could watch out for each other. In my mind, I had a constant fight between right and wrong. Then, at the Catholic school, the nuns kept telling us that even a thought about kissing a boy was sinful. No wonder my younger sisters married too young to older men and in a short period of time! Well, at least we all did well in life and had our families.

It was almost Thanksgiving when a horrible snowstorm hit our city. It was the first time we had ever seen snow! My father called us to the living room window of our apartment at 6:00 a.m. so we could see our street and lawns covered by snow. Everything was white! We could not see our car because it was also covered by snow. It was an impressive sight.

Thank God we did not have to go to work that day, but we needed to scrape the snow off our car right away. Later on, we went outside and began playing in the snow. In the pictures below, my father and Aunt Marta are shoveling the snow, and my mother almost fell. It was freezing! My niece Maria Elena was enjoying the snow with a friend, while Maria Elena's mother, Marita, and my mother were watching them.

After this break, we went back to work. I rode every day with my aunt since, as you know, we were working at the same school. Besides that, I never drove under those conditions. We had to defrost and clean the car's windshield before leaving. The temperature was still below freezing! She had the engine on, warming the car, while we scraped off the snow. My aunt was already kind of getting used to this climate. In our case, we were still adjusting to it.

Nighttime came too early for us, by 4:00 to 4:30 p.m., which I found depressing. The city was hilly, and if the roads were icy, you had to know how to control your car or risk having an accident. I was afraid to drive at night on the icy roads with dangerous cliffs. Also, the winters there were brutal! Icy roads and snowstorms made driving very dangerous.

One day, I took my mother and sisters Julita and Mirtica shopping. When we came out of the store, it was dark and snowing. We could not find my car. All the cars were covered by snow! When we first arrived in June, we had laughed and wondered why everybody had a flower or a flag at the end of their cars' antennas. I surely needed one too that night!

Finally, we found the car, and while I was driving those hilly roads, I could not see well or distinguish the edge of the road. I almost drove off a cliff! I had never driven on icy and snowy pavement before! It was too dangerous for me to drive under those conditions.

A policeman saw what happened just as I stopped. He approached my car, told me to roll down the window and advised me that I needed to park the car during winter; otherwise, I was going to kill someone or be killed. He helped me to back out and get back on the road.

We all loved to watch television programs like *Benny Hill* and *Hee Haw*. My parents laughed a lot while watching them since they did not have to know much English to understand what was happening.

I loved watching concerts by Tom Jones and Engelbert Humperdinck. They were the famous ones at that time. Other bands' music was too strident for my taste. I went to a nightclub with Milton and my sisters, but the music was too loud for us. We did some dancing and left right away.

Another day, Milton invited Julita and me to go to a nice nightclub. When we got there, another friend was there too. We all went to the entrance, and they had to pay a cover charge to enter. We were enjoying a drink when the curtain on the stage opened to reveal an all-women band. When they began playing, I could not believe what I was seeing; those women were topless. Right away, I told Julita that we were leaving. The guys were surprised too! We all left, and the ride back home with Milton was very quiet.

In February 1972, Julita married Milton. It was a nice, intimate civil ceremony at our home. My mother and grandmother cooked all the Cuban menu. We invited a few friends to come, and Milton's family came from New York to be with us on this occasion. It was a happy moment, and they looked very in love. They went to New York City for their honeymoon, but the other married sisters and cousins went with them too and stayed at the same hotel. They enjoyed visiting New York City, all the night life, and its people.

Going back to school one morning, when the students came into the classroom, I noticed that one of the kids had a black-and-blue mark on his neck. I thought this child had been abused, so I asked him, "What happened?" He said it was a hickey. I did not know the meaning of that word, but I knew what it was. Then Teddy asked me what he said, and I told him in a very low tone of voice. We did not know if this mark was truly what the child said it was or if this child had been abused in one way or another. Too young to know what that was! Deep inside of me, I knew I had to learn those words to keep out of trouble.

It was frustrating trying to help those students who were aware of my weakness. Later, the last day of that week, I was called to the principal's office. He was informed by Teddy that I did not know the meaning of bad words or some idiomatic expressions of the English language. I had never learned those words in Cuba or at the college I was attending. Therefore, the principal assigned a Puerto-Rican teacher, Sonia, to tutor me in all the bad words and idioms used in this country. She even gave me a book of American idioms, which I still have. We laughed together about my ignorance of those words. We became very close; surely, she helped me to understand local expressions and how a word can change its meaning if you do not pronounce it correctly.

The following week, I noticed one of the students, Luis, was playing with a nice toy, a small car. Amicably, I asked him where he got it, or where his mom purchased it. To my surprise, his answer in Spanish was that his mother told him to steal it, so he did. I explained to him that such actions were wrong, that he could go to jail for doing something like that. His answer was that he thought nothing was wrong with stealing the car since his own mother had told him to do it. What kind of mother was that, teaching her child to steal? I felt so sad because I could not change his mind. Now, I wonder what has become of that cute child?

I wanted to be accepted and to be like other Americans, dress as they dressed. As I mentioned before, the style then was to wear miniskirts, boots, tight bodysuits, no bras—you know, the hippies' style. Well, I purchased some nice outfits in the clearance basement of a known store there. We could not afford anything expensive. My figure then was right for that type of clothing; I was in shape, young, and pretty. I was very attractive because I looked different and acted unlike most Americans. Many of the guys in college wanted to meet me when they heard my accent. "Who is this new girl?!"

Teddy always invited me to go places in town, and even skiing with a group of teachers from our school during spring break. My parents did not let me go out of town alone. "Too much temptation!" they said. During the summer vacation, Teddy went on a trip to Europe and brought me nice gifts: a beautiful Spanish doll and French books, so I could practice my French and keep it alive. I still have those books and can get by with the French I learned in school and still remember.

One morning, I was again called to the principal's office. This time, it was his secretary and another teacher who wanted to speak to me. His secretary told me that my provocative way of dressing was not appropriate for the school's code of conduct. I was wearing a miniskirt with thick tights underneath, so you could not see the skin of my legs, boots, and a long-sleeve body shirt. At that moment I thought, *The only provocative things are my big breasts.*

I looked at both and asked, "Are you ladies wearing a bra?"

They each answered, "No, I am not." They were not as full-breasted as I was, but, still, you could see their nipples.

I responded, "You see, I am wearing one." Since we were close in age, I continued by asking them, "Are you living with your parents?"

Again, each answered, "No, I live with my boyfriend."

So I said to them, "Well, I am still a virgin, I do not have a boyfriend, and I live with my parents."

They both looked at each other, then at me. The secretary told me to forget about this conversation and go back to my classroom.

During lunchtime, I told Teddy what happened that morning and how embarrassed I was. He told me that those ladies were jealous of my beauty because they did not have the attributes I had. We were really wearing the same outfits in a way, but mine was attractive on me. I really appreciated Teddy's words of encouragement. He surely was a good friend, and I was very thankful for his friendship. Anyways, the school year was almost over, and we needed to concentrate on our students' progress instead of trivial things.

At the end of June 1972, when my cousin Mayito was authorized his first military leave, he married his girlfriend, Tina, in New Jersey. We were all invited to attend their wedding. The problem was that we did not have anything nice to wear. My aunt Marta took us to the basement of this famous store in town again, and there we found beautiful long dresses on the clearance rack. We tried them on, and we were thrilled to see they fit us just right. It seems these were prom dresses the store wanted to get rid of. We were very lucky!

The other problem was where to stay in New Jersey while attending the wedding. We were a large group of people without any money to pay for a hotel room. We were so happy that Tina's family—who happened to be first cousins of Magaly, my cousin Chito's wife—invited some of us to stay in their relatives' houses, which were not too far from each other. My immediate family stayed at the home of Fina, Magaly's mom. We were lucky and thankful for our family's support at all times.

The wedding was beautiful, and we all looked fabulous in our new clothes. My cousin and his bride were so in love. It was our first church wedding in the USA, especially since it was someone dear to us getting married. We were all so very happy that my cousin would no longer feel lonely from being away from his mother and grandmother. They were a young couple ready for a new life at the US Army base in California. When Mayito finished his service in the army, they moved to Miami and purchased a house not too far from us. We were all together again, except for his mother and grandmother who were still up north.

Teachers formed a soccer team. I asked permission to have a cheerleading group, and it was approved. Some of the girls became very excited about the idea of cheering for their team. I made the pom-poms, and we practiced half an hour after school with the team. Parents were happy their children were outdoors exercising and socializing. Teddy and Tony were the coaches of our team. We went to all the games, and it was a lot of fun to cheer for our school team.

The City of Worcester was celebrating its 250th anniversary. We had a school meeting in which the principal asked for our help in organizing a program that represented our school. I offered to help organize a presentation of dances from different countries. The school had students from Colombia, Costa Rica, Cuba, Ecuador, Panama, Dominican Republic, Puerto Rico, and others. The students' parents were excited about their children participating in this important community event. They cooperated by making their costumes and bringing the music. I prepared the choreography and got them ready for their presentations. They practiced after school with the consent of their parents and at home. How proud were those parents when they saw their children doing the typical dances that represented their countries!

Our school was commended in different newspapers for our beautiful presentation and the great job the students did dancing to their typical music, wearing their native costumes, and delivering a great program for the entertainment of all the people attending this special ceremony. Our principal was congratulated in the news for the nice display of typical music representing different nationalities. This made me very happy. What a successful program we had!

In July, we went to the beach in Maine with some friends. We were so happy when we saw and smelled the sea, but we were very surprised that nobody was in the water. We had missed going to the beach! As soon as we got there, we ran into the water and stopped right away when the water got to just our ankles. Oh no, the water was freezing! We got out of it as fast as we went in. Our toes were turning purple! What a disappointment! Thank God there were rides, including a Ferris wheel, at this beach entertainment park. There was also a restaurant where we had lunch and used their facility. We had a great time even though we could not go swimming. We were not going to let the disappointment that we could not swim get us down. We needed to make this one a nice trip, and we did.

One weekend, we went to Boston, rode around the city sightseeing, and had a picnic in a park, eating sandwiches we made at home. The guys brought a cooler with sodas and water. They were not drinkers, thank God. We were all short of cash since our friends were studying at the university, and the money they were getting from their parents was not enough sometimes. It was understandable since we did not have enough money either, or none of us could count on help from our parents. We were young and could not let this stop us from enjoying life, so we found entertainment in cheap ways. Picnicking!

A year had already passed since we arrived in the USA. We were counting our blessings, but still thinking about the wintertime we had just experienced. We were not used to that type of weather. We loved the spring, the summer, and some parts of autumn, but not the heavy snowfall of our first Thanksgiving in the US. We missed Cuba's tropical weather and the beach. We also missed my sister Julita, who was already living in Miami, and she missed us.

My parents visited some Cuban friends who lived in Springfield. Their son was the emcee of a Spanish television program in 1972, which was shown live on the local channel 40. We were even invited to sing some Cuban songs on this program. I sang while my sister Mirtica accompanied me on the piano. The songs we interpreted were *"Pensando en Tí," "Y si Mañana,"* and "Guantanamera." We wore the beautiful long dresses we purchased for my cousin's wedding. Unfortunately, their son died the following year from brain cancer. I believe he was only thirty years old.

I will always remember the first time we arrived in the USA and the city of Worcester, which offered us the help we needed at that crucial moment of our lives. We met very nice people and made good memories, which will stay in our minds forever. Even though all these good things were happening, we missed the tropical climate of Cuba and the beach. Winters were too long and too cold for all of us in Massachusetts; they depressed us. We needed a change of climate!

Chapter 4

MOVING TO MIAMI

The end of the school year came, and we were ready to enjoy the summer. Julita was in Miami with her husband when my mother, Mirtica, and I decided to visit them. We did so in August 1972. After arriving there, we fell in love with the bubbling city, the sparkling lights at night, the sunny days, and especially the warm beaches. As soon as we arrived there, we felt as if we were home.

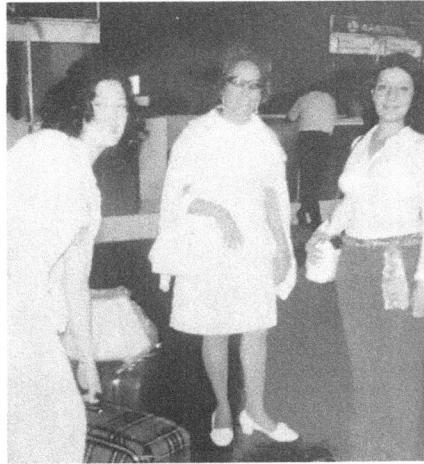

We met with some of our friends who had left Cuba several years before us. Miami seemed like a progressive place, and the enjoyment of being around people like us was overwhelming. Up north, we had gone through a rough winter with a lot of snowstorms; we did not want to experience that again. Even though we still had close family up there—my sisters Marita and Margarita with their families, my grandmother, and my aunt—we did not wish to return.

Instead, my mother began talking to our family members up north and encouraging them to move to Miami. My mother called my father and told him that we were staying in Miami; if he wanted to continue being married to her, he needed to move down south.

This picture of me was taken when we went to Miami Beach for the first time. We went by bus since Julita's husband was using the only car they had, and mine was up north. The ride was enjoyable though, and we loved looking at a new panorama. When we arrived at the beach, we could not hold ourselves back; we immediately ran into the water. We were very happy to enjoy the beach again.

Later, some friends whom we had not seen in many years joined us there. We loved seeing them while enjoying the beach, talking about Cuba and all our friends who were still there or had left the island before us, having a wonderful time under the sun, and breathing in the happiness of finally being free. We were full of hope that we were going to have a better future here in Miami…and we did, thank God.

Finally, my father decided to leave the North and join us in Miami. Then, I called the school and told them of my decision to stay in Miami. But it was too overwhelming for him to dismantle the entire house alone. He did not know what to do with all the things we left behind, including my car; therefore, I offered to go back there and help him move. It was the first week of September, and school was getting ready to begin when I flew to Massachusetts.

First thing I did when I got there was go to the school where I was working to say goodbye and thank them for all their support and friendship. I expressed to the school principal how thankful I was for all the help he offered me. Teddy organized a beautiful going-away party at a gorgeous house which belonged to a friend. My grand-mother and Aunt Marta also gave us a going-away party at their home, where some of our school friends joined us too. I was so thankful for those who had given helping hands when we arrived in pursuit of the freedom of this great country that has a different language and culture into which we would have to learn to assimilate. At the same time, it was sad to leave behind my two sisters, Marita and Margarita, with their families. Well, at least they were living in the same building. It was also sad to leave Grand-mother Aurora and Aunt Marta. But we had to do what we had to do; otherwise, we all would still be up there.

My father and I had a lot to do to empty the apartment. At cheap prices, we sold all the furniture and other things that we were not going to need, making only a total of $500. We sent the piano with a moving company. Many other things were given to our family and friends living there. We gathered all the clothing and household items—like sheets, blankets, and kitchen stuff—that we were going to need at our new place in Miami and loaded them into the car. Soon, we were ready to go back to the sunny, tropical weather of Miami, Florida. We were worried about the uncertainty of finding jobs right away because we did not have the money to support ourselves or set up a house. But deep down inside, we knew everything was going to be all right.

When my father and I finally arrived in Miami, the next thing we had to do was to find a place to live. We were lucky that we found one right away, not too far from the one Julita and Milton were renting. Rent then was low, so we were able to pay the deposit plus the first month's rent, turn on the electricity and water, have a phone line installed, and buy groceries for the first week at our new place. After that, our precious $500 was gone!

We begged the owner to leave the existing sectional sofa in the living room and the small table with four chairs in the kitchen. My parents then went with some friends from Cuba to buy a bedroom set using this couple's credit. They knew my parents so well that they trusted them with their credit line. Mirtica and I slept on the sectional sofa in the living room since we did not have any money left with which to buy beds for us. We needed to work ASAP!

Our father found a job at a store as a salesman right away. I got a job in the accounting department of a wholesale industrial equipment distribution company, and Mirtica became a teller in a bank nearby. Julita was already working at a laundromat and Milton at a dental laboratory since that was his career. A few years later, he opened his own dental lab. Surely luck was on our side!

Our sister Marita was feeling lonely up north, away from us. She and her husband decided to move to Miami to be near us. The owner of the house we were renting had another house behind ours; it was a little bit bigger and had two bedrooms, two bathrooms, big living and dining areas, plus a porch that had been converted into a family room. We decided to move there so we could all live together.

I gave Mirtica a ride to work, and my father rode with a friend. One day, while coming home from work, the block before ours, I saw that someone had thrown away two twin mattresses and their box springs. We stopped and asked if we could take them. The people were so glad to get rid of that old junk that, with their help, we put them on the top of my car and tied them down. They also gave us a chest of drawers and an old armchair that we had to find a way to transport later that day. Mirtica and I had all what we needed in our bedroom! We bought mattress covers, so we did not sleep directly on top of the old, used mattresses. We already had our own sheets, pillows, and blankets we had brought from up north. When we knew that Marita and her family were coming, we bought a sleeper sofa for the family room for her and Roly; then someone gave us a twin bed for Maria Elenita, who was six at the time. Our house was all set!

They arrived before Thanksgiving 1972 to celebrate it with us. Immediately, they looked for jobs and a place to live. Marita began working in the accounting department of a shipping company in the same building where I worked. Roly got a job as a salesman in a warehouse. My mother babysat for her granddaughter Maria Elenita when she came home from school each day. I drove Mirtica and Marita to work.

Margarita stayed up north. She had a son, Frankie, and they were afraid to make the move without the security of having a job. Eventually, Marita and Roly found a duplex half a block from ours. Then, Julita and Milton moved from their apartment to a house across the street from Marita's. My parents were overwhelmed at having almost all their daughters surrounding them again.

Christmas came, and we celebrated it all together...of course, missing the rest of the family who were left behind. We were so thankful that we had places to live, jobs, and wonderful times with many friends who had left Cuba before us, people we had not seen in years. It was great to enjoy the freedom this country offered, the very thing we had lost in Cuba. We came to the US with the mentality that it was going to take hard work and study to achieve our dreams, but we were free and ready to take on the challenge. To learn English was a priority too!

It was time for me to continue college. I had to decide what field I wanted to study. After working eight hours in the accounting department of my company each day, I went to school. My decision was made; I wanted to revalidate my teaching credentials, not pursue a degree in accounting. So that was what I did. The owner of the company was not too happy when he heard that, but it was my life, and that was the path I wanted to take. I love math, but I also love teaching. Even though I was making a good salary at this distribution company, I felt that teaching was a more challenging job. Sharing knowledge and dealing with students was exciting to me and much preferable to sitting behind a desk for hours.

What a surprise! Margarita called and said that she was coming to spend some days with us. It was February 1973. Mima had been talking to Margarita about how much she missed them, so Margarita decided to come and visit. She came with Frankie, whom we had not met yet; he was only a few months old. They stayed on the sleeper sofa in the family room, and someone lent us a crib for the baby. We surely enjoyed having them around, and at the same time, we were sad because Margarita was going up north. Even though she loved Miami, Margarita missed her husband.

One morning after dropping Mirtica at her job, I hit the back of a bus in front of me when it suddenly stopped in traffic. I got out of the car to check the damage just as the bus driver took off with my bumper attached to the bus's bumper, dragging my car behind the bus. He had not even noticed that I hit him! Marita, who was riding in my car, began screaming. I ran beside the bus, yelling to the bus driver to stop. He stopped, and I told him what happened. He got out of the bus and saw then that my car's bumper was attached to the bus. He lifted the front of my car, detaching it from the bus, and told me that it was nothing, to forget about it. Thank God nothing happened, and we continued the drive to work. Now we laugh about this incident, but we were very scared at the time.

I must tell you about something that happened at work. The owner of the distribution company where I was working called me to his office to tell me that I needed to buy a new car because mine was old and looked awful parked in front of the building; he felt it made his company look bad. He offered to lend me the car's down payment from his business; I could pay it back from my weekly salary. He referred me to see his friend, who had an auto dealership, for help in finding a nice car. The monthly payments on the car loan were not that bad since the interest rate was very low then. I bought a nice blue Chevy Malibu! I was so happy that I purchased a new car, and I loved its smell. Driving it was even nicer. Marita also loved it and enjoyed riding with me. I was so thankful to the owner of my company for the help in buying the new car. I later found out he had given the same opportunity to two other employees. The company's parking lot looked so nice! Around that time, I was moved to another position and became assistant to the comptroller. One of my Cuban friends, Bea, was hired as the bookkeeper.

A Cuban friend of the family, Juan, came to visit us, and when he saw Mirtica, he fell in love with her. He was getting divorced and had two children from his previous marriage. My father thought that Juan was going to fall in love with me because I was older and single. But, no, it was the youngest one. So I was going to be the only one single, living with my parents. I was so involved in work and school that I did not have time for anything else. Juan and my sister were married in December and moved into an apartment in the northwest area of Miami.

A year after Margarita's visit, in February 1974, she; her husband, Frank; and Frankie moved to Miami. My parents were so happy to have all their girls, plus the two grandchildren, together again. We found a house for them in the same block as Marita's and Julita's houses. We could walk to their places and enjoy Sunday barbecues, birthday parties, etc. My mother babysat for Frankie. Margarita's husband, Frank, began working as a salesman at the same company as Roly. She got a job as a teller at a nearby bank. We were all working, and I was going to college to get my teaching certificate in the USA.

In May 1974, I graduated from college with a bachelor's degree in liberal arts and a teaching certification with a major in Spanish. I continued working at the distribution company since my salary was great. I was glad the hard days of working and going to college full time were over. It took a lot of sacrifice, but I was able to accomplish my goal. My family was very proud of me because I was the first one in the family to receive a degree in the United States of America. I continued working as an assistant to the comptroller at the wholesale distribution company until May 1975, when I decided it was time for me to seek a new job in the career I had studied for and was certified in. Years later, while teaching, I went back to major in mathematics since the accounting degree helped me with that.

During those years, Miami was still very Americanized. The stores were owned by Americans, and you could not find many Spanish markets. Years later, Cubans began opening their own businesses and bringing in Spanish merchandise for the Latin American consumers. It was as if Miami was waking up from the sleepy city it had been. Buildings began going up, and you could see how much the city was progressing because of the Cuban migration. Years later, there were a lot of immigrants from Central America, like Nicaraguans, and South America, like Venezuelans, after these countries fell under the control of Communist regimes. The political situation in those countries brought to the US a lot of people fleeing the Socialist/Communist doctrine. Spanish was, and still is, the language spoken in all those new businesses. If you visit Miami today, it feels as if you were in a Latin American country. You need to speak Spanish to survive in some areas!

In the beginning of 1975, while watching television, I saw an advertisement for new houses in a city south of Miami. My parents and I went to check them out and find out about their cost. When we told the rest of the family, they all wanted to see them too. They fell in love with the area and the houses' large lots; the kids could enjoy the outdoors there. They all decided to purchase houses in that neighborhood. The down payments were only $250 dollars per house, and the houses cost from the high twenties to the high thirties in terms of thousands of dollars. I used my income tax check to pay for my parents' down payment. Their mortgage payments were about what they were paying in rent. Unbelievable!

Chapter 5

Achieving
the American Dream!

In 1975, we purchased our new houses in Leisure City, all on the same block: my parents' house was first, then Marita's, Margarita's, and Julita's. Mirtica's house was at the end of the street, on the cul-de-sac. In four years, we were achieving the American dream of being owners of our own homes! We knew that our commute was going to take a little bit longer, but we were so happy that we did not care about the driving. Marita, Mirtica, and I rode together to save gasoline. Julita began working in the office of a nearby farm. Margarita, Frank, and Roly rode together. My father worked as a janitor at a school in Florida City. At this time, we all had cars too!

Later that year, I quit my job at the distribution company. I wanted to work in my career, so I began looking for a teaching position right away. I heard from one of our new neighbors, my dear friend Carmen, that the adult center nearby was looking for a teacher. I made an appointment with the school principal, and she sent me to the school department's main office in downtown Miami for an interview.

When I got there, there was a panel of three of the adult centers' administrators ready to ask me questions. I answered them all, and it seemed they liked my responses since I got the teaching position. I was going to be dealing with a lot of migrant students who lived in the area, and they needed someone who spoke Spanish too. I was fluent in Spanish, English, and French. There were only a few daytime adult centers in the county, and I was lucky to get a job at one of them. I began with a part-time contract, and a few years later, it was upgraded to a continuing contract.

The school was in an old building in the downtown area of Homestead, near a lot of restaurants and stores. There was another adult center close by, in another building. Most of the students were from Central and South America, and they were farmworkers. They were in a government program that paid them to go to school to be trained in a skill while learning English. Mine was a daytime position in the learning lab, which was what the classroom was called. There were two teachers assigned to the learning lab. The other teacher decided that I should teach the math part; she wanted to teach the reading and language parts of the adult basic-education curriculum, which was based on open-entry, open-exit multilevel enrollment. This meant that in a classroom, there were students at different educational and learning levels, and they came and left at different times. For example, you could not stand in front of the entire class and use the blackboard to teach addition and subtraction of whole numbers because some students were already working with fractions, decimals, etc. The first thing we as teachers had to do was to give each student an entry exam to determine their level—beginning, middle, or advanced—and from there, to decide what were the weak areas on which they needed to focus.

Some of the students were illiterate, either because they never went to school, because of some form of learning disability, or they had never received any formal education in their native language. We had other students who had degrees in their countries or simply dropped out of high school. That was the situation we were dealing with in this classroom.

After the entry exam, we had to write an individualized lesson plan based on the questions the student got wrong on the test. The instruction had to be individualized to reinforce their weak areas. In one class, I had students dealing with anything from simple whole numbers, to fractions, to decimals, and all the way up to algebra. If several students were weak in the same area, then you worked with them in a small group without disturbing the rest of the students who were working in other areas independently.

Most of the students were from different Spanish-speaking countries, others were Black, and White students were in the minority. The way math was taught in Spanish-speaking countries was the same way I learned it in Cuba; therefore, it was much better for me to work with those students. I always told my students that it did not matter how they worked the problem if, at the end, the answer was correct. I took the math books home, and at night, I studied the way math was taught in the United States since I also had some American students in the classroom. In Latin America, students are taught using the metric system, which has not been adopted by the USA yet.

In those years, we did not have the technology we have today, so I needed to personally give individualized instruction. We used audiovisual tapes and tape players, which went along with the lesson in a book or on a handout. When teaching a group, we used the overhead projector with transparencies. We also used sound cards for the students with limited English proficiency, so they could repeat the word as many times as they needed.

Every day, before the class started, all students stood up to say the Pledge of Allegiance, sing the national anthem and pause for a moment of silent meditation. Then, I did not know the pledge or the hymn; I had to memorize them in order to guide my students. To my surprise, some of the American students did not know them either, so I made copies of the words so they could read them aloud. There was one student who practiced a religion which forbade them from pledging to any flag; therefore, she took this moment to go to the restroom. It was a solemn moment, especially when everybody silently said their own prayers or simply enjoyed a moment of silence.

There was a very knowledgeable, perfectly bilingual (Spanish and English) teacher who taught English as a Second Language (ESL). I admired him because he surely knew his subject well and encouraged all the students to speak the new language. Since my classroom was next to the principal's office, sometimes I could hear her when she was speaking loudly. One day, I heard the principal having a heated argument with one of the teachers. It was the ESL teacher! He was so upset with the principal that he simply walked out of the school and left. I could not believe it! Such an intelligent person walking away from a job like ours. He lacked the patience and tolerance to deal with his superior. Our students really lost a great teacher that day.

During one of our planning days, we had to go to an adult-education meeting at the school department's main building in downtown Miami. To my surprise, I found this teacher working there. He was doing a great job in the administration building, dealing with the adult basic-education program. I was so happy to see him there and glad that his talent was not being wasted. Maybe it was best for him to walk away from the circumstances at our school. We were dealing with a very authoritarian principal. She showed me her true colors later in my career.

My sisters began having children, and life was settled for all of us. My mother began selling houses at a construction company nearby. She purchased a car, learned how to drive, and drove herself to work every day. By then, she was fifty-three years old.

In August of the same year, I met the man of my life, my future husband, Bob. His American family owned the gas station where we purchased our fuel and where my father worked years later while Bob was managing it and doing mechanical work. My parents were very happy that we fell in love. They knew I was marrying a good man.

When Bob and I met, it was as if we were made for each other. Bob knew my dad before he met me, and Bob spoke to him in Spanish when my dad drove into the gas station. One day, Bob noticed my father driving my car and figured that I must be his daughter. Bob says he fell in love with me the first time he saw me drive into his station. From then on, when I drove in, Bob's brothers and sisters made sure he knew I was coming so he could fill up my gas tank, clean my windshield, and, of course, speak with me.

Let me tell you how we met. One day, when I got to the gas station, Bob ran to service my car; he cleaned my windshield while putting gas in the tank. At one point, he came to the driver's window and began talking to me. He told me that he was going down to the Keys to fish for lobster. I told him that I loved lobster. He then invited me for dinner at a restaurant that served lobster.

At the time, I happened to be on my way to a doctor in Miami because I had a lump in my breast. The doctor looked at me and told me that I needed to go to the hospital for a biopsy the next day. So, that night, I called Bob and told him that I was sorry, but I could not go out with him for dinner that Saturday because I was having a lumpectomy. He asked me what the name of the hospital was, and I told him.

The next day, when I woke from surgery, my mother said, "Nery, wake up; you got a bouquet of beautiful red roses, and we don't know who sent them."

The card said, "Love you, Bob." At that point, I could not think of who Bob was. A few minutes later, I remembered it was the guy from the gas station. Bob called me that night, and I told him that I was going home the next day. He came to my home that Sunday and brought me a box of chocolates. That was so sweet of him.

While we were dating, Bob came to see me every night after closing the gas station. He had already finished college when his father offered him the job at his business. He invited me to go with him to the wedding of his older brother, Jay, in October. I accepted the invitation and looked for a nice dress at a reasonable price. It was a long red dress. We were seated at the main table since Bob was the best man. After the wedding, the bride, Barbara, told me that she was surprised I was wearing red at the wedding because, to Americans, that meant the bride was not a virgin. I was not aware of this custom! I told her that it was not my intention to offend her. On the contrary, I was so happy for them and proud to be part of this family. She understood after my apology.

One day, my grandmother sat in the living room, petting the cat while chaperoning us. I begged her to go to bed and told her we were old enough to know what we were doing. My mother said the same thing to her. But my grandmother refused to leave; she stayed and fell asleep while waiting for Bob to leave.

Another day, Bob came over wearing cutoffs with strings hanging down his legs. My grandmother offered me money so I could go to the store and purchase this poor guy new pants. I explained to her that it was the fashion. She could not believe it and insisted, but I reassured her that it was the style, that he did not need any money. Funny!

There are eight siblings in Bob's family. While dating, we used to visit his parents on Sundays; his brothers, sisters, and Aunt Margaret were always there. His sister Barbara suffered from cerebral palsy caused by the doctor using forceps during her birth; he squeezed too hard and damaged a part of her brain. The youngest, Mike, was still in elementary school. He is twenty years younger than Bob! When they were all together, they always talked about things that were happening at the gas station. Even though Bob's sisters, Mary Lou and Nancy, were going to college, they worked at the gas station during the summer and school breaks. His brother Ray was still going to high school, and after class and when there was no school, and sometimes in the evenings, he worked at the gas station too. Jay and Rick were already married, and they worked at the gas station full time, as did Bob.

During one of the Sunday gatherings, one of his sisters said, "Do you remember that old lady with the green Chevy?"

Bob said, "Yes, I remember her."

She continued, "She kicked the bucket!"

Then I said, "Why did she kick the bucket?"

Everybody began laughing like crazy. I was wondering about what I just said, but Bob explained to me that it meant she died. Oh well, I did not learn that idiom in college.

Another time when we were talking, Bob said that the guy they were talking about was a douche bag. When I went to the kitchen, his mom asked me who they were talking about. Aunt Margaret was there too when I told Bob's mother what he said.

Mom's eyes and mouth opened so big. Aunt Margaret got upset and told me not to repeat that. Then she went to where the group was and told them not to use that type of vocabulary in front of me without explaining its meaning. It was a very embarrassing moment!

Christmas came, and to my surprise, Bob gave me a beautiful engagement ring. When I showed it to his father, he asked me, "When is the wedding?"

I was very surprised because we had not talked about a wedding, and my answer was that I did not know. He could not believe I did not know.

Then Bob said, "In June."

I was so surprised to hear this. His father explained to me that when an American man gives a ring to his girlfriend, it means that he is going to marry her. I told him that, in Cuba, it meant that the relationship was getting serious, and it could be years before there is talk of marriage.

By January, Bob asked me when I was going to begin planning the wedding. I told him that I thought the man planned the wedding and reception; that's how it was done in Cuba. He explained to me that, in America, it was the bride's family who was in charge of that. I only had $1,000 saved, and the rest of my family did not have anything after the purchase of their new homes and furniture. Bob and I then decided to plan and pay for the wedding ourselves and not involve our families. I was lucky to find a bridal store in downtown Miami that was going out of business. I bought a beautiful wedding dress there for $300; I still have it.

Bob had saved $10,000, which was a lot of money then. We purchased one of the homes my mother was selling in January 1976, and it was almost finished when we got married in June of the same year. We were very fortunate because a furniture store was closing its doors, and Bob was able to purchase the living room, bedroom, and dining room furniture there. They also held it at the store until the house was ready the following month. It took four months after our wedding for the house to be finished though.

We were thrilled that everything was falling into place and that we were going to have a brand-new home and the wedding of our dreams. A beautiful white gown, bridesmaids, the church and banquet hall beautifully decorated, a professional photographer and even a band to play at the reception. We were lucky to do it all on our limited budget.

My parents and all my sisters were so happy that I was finally getting married. I was the last Barnet girl still single, so they could not wait for me to do it. Bob and I fell in love, and we were ready to be married and enjoy our life together. It was something that was meant to happen, as if we had been waiting for each other. We made a life commitment!

My mother's English was limited, but at least my father was able to communicate with Bob's family. My mother told us that she was never good with languages. Even when she studied English while attending elementary and secondary school at St. Vincent de Paul School in Cuba, she struggled with it. She even began taking English lessons at a college during the evening, but she just couldn't learn it. I guess some people are that way with languages.

In June, we got married at the Sacred Heart Catholic Church in Homestead. My sister Marita was the maid of honor, and Bob's older brother, Jay, was his best man. My sister Julita was one of the bridesmaids, and her husband's niece Maria the other one. My cousin Mayito and Bob's brother Ray were the groomsmen. My niece Maria Elena and Lizzie, the daughter of my friend Beatriz, were the flower girls while Mario—her son, also my godson—was the ring bearer.

Two of my sisters did not want to be bridesmaids because Margarita was pregnant with Lily and Mirtica with Vivian. Years later, Margarita had another daughter, Liset, and Mirtica had a son, Ricky. Julita, who already had Javier, then had Milton, Jr. Marita's son, Guille, was only a year old at the time.

My father was very happy that he was walking his last daughter down the aisle. Finally, my parents were glad to have all their daughters in homes of their own and starting their own families. We invited 200 people, so we had a good group there. The band played great music, and everybody had a lot of fun. After the wedding, we went on a Caribbean cruise for our honeymoon. After the cruise, we continued to honeymoon for another week, visiting different places while driving around Florida.

Chapter 6

MARRIED LIFE AND NEW SCHOOL VISION

As I said before, in June we had our dream wedding at the Homestead Air Force Base NCO Club, thanks to one of our friends who was a member there. We were able to contract a band to play the music. We had a beautiful three-layer cake with a fountain. We also had a champagne fountain. The price for the reception was low because it was at the Homestead Air Force Base; otherwise, its cost would have been unbelievable.

Our cute new house had a split-bedroom plan. The master bedroom and bathroom were on one side of the house, and the three other bedrooms and bath were on the opposite end of the home. We converted one of the bedrooms into a den in which to watch television. Living and dining rooms were combined in a large room, with the kitchen to one side and the den to the other. A few years later, we built a large screened porch in the back for parties. The house sat on a large lot; we were ready to have our children grow up there.

During our honeymoon, Bob and I talked about starting a family. We did not want to wait too long! Two months after our wedding, I found out that I was pregnant with our first child. We were thrilled with this grand news! One night, I had to go to the restroom. When I sat down, I fell all the way into the toilet bowl because Bob had left the seat up. After this happened, I started bleeding. I could not believe I might lose the baby! The doctor told me to rest more, just to be on the safe side. I stayed home and rested for a month. Lucky me that I was able to do that.

Finally, our new house was ready, and we needed to move into it. Thank God for my sister Margarita and her husband, Frank, who came to help us. It was in a nice, brand-new neighborhood, not too far from my parents' and sisters' homes and our jobs. Also, it was not too far from Bob's parents. We had already purchased new furniture, we had nice drapes installed, and the house really looked beautiful. For our wedding, we had received beautiful gifts of silver, which went right into the dining room's open hutch styled to match our colonial furniture. It was not my taste, but it was what Bob wanted for our home. Life in freedom was a dream coming true!

The new school building was done too! It was a nice structure in which the following skills were taught: automotive technology, air-conditioning repair, building maintenance, clerical and administrative-assistant training, and child care. Later, the program for nurse's aides was added. Each skill had its own classroom and shop. Besides that, the school had five additional class-rooms, a learning lab, a library, and a cafeteria. It also had the main office and a teachers' lounge. There was also a large office on the first floor of the building, across from the main office, for the migrant workers' program, which was part of the school department. All the teachers were so happy to be in this beautiful building with new furniture, everything so neat and clean. Teachers from other adult centers envied us! The school had day and night shifts. I was lucky to continue working the day shift, especially with my pregnancy.

My classroom was called the learning lab. It was large and had cubicles along the walls and two more rows back-to-back for more students. Students, who were already studying a skill, were assigned an hour in the learning lab to continue studying and improving their reading skills, practicing English and math, or getting ready to take the general equivalency diploma test (GED). The classroom had a new computer in each cubicle and two desks, one at each end of the room, for the teachers. All the audiovisual materials, books, and storage cabinets were housed in a small room next to the classroom. We had an aide who helped us keep everything in order.

A new teacher, Larry, was assigned to work with me in this beautiful learning lab. He was of Mexican descent. Our assistant was Maria from Cuba. We were all young and very enthusiastic bilingual teachers, English and Spanish. Next to our classroom was the English for Speakers of

Other Languages (ESOL) classroom. The teacher was a retired, old Black gentleman who was able to speak some Spanish. I am not sure about his background, but the students respected him, and some were afraid of him because he told them he practiced voodoo. This classroom was joined to ours by a door, so if he needed to go to the office or restroom, he opened the door between the classrooms and asked us to watch his students.

Later in the year, Maria's husband had an awful accident on US 41 coming from Naples. He suffered a spinal-cord injury that required surgery, which was successful, but he could not walk for over a year. Maria had to stop working and take care of him and their daughters. Our great team was gone!

Later, Larry transferred to another school closer to home. A new teacher was assigned to work in the learning lab with me. He was glad I was dealing with math, which was my favorite subject anyway. We made a good team with a new assistant; a young Mexican girl, Tomasita, began helping us.

When the adult basic-education program was computerized, we teachers had to be trained in the use of the computers first; then we had to train the students on how to use them. The computerized system was called PLATO. It was the latest innovation in adult basic education. It was an intense training, but at the end, we knew how to work all the wonderful programs. It was the best thing for our individualized open-entry, open-exit style of teaching. We were thrilled with this new technology. At this point, we were sharing the teaching of all the three subjects: reading, language, and math.

We always tried to sanitize the computers before a new group of students came into the lab. Sometimes, even the students helped with this task. Remember, we were dealing with adults. All students were given a placement test; then we had to write an individualized instruction plan for each of them and place it in an easily accessible folder so the students could keep track of their assignments and modular tests and know when to move to the next topic. We were very busy the entire day, keeping track of their lessons and helping them with their assignments. The ESOL students came for an hour during their teachers' planning time.

Bob was managing the gas station and doing some of the mechanical work there. He came home for dinner, but he had to go back to close the business. Sometimes I went with him. I also went to see him after work since the school was only one block away. One day, I got to the station just in time to see Bob getting into a car with a young, pretty Asian lady. She moved just enough to let Bob squeeze in and drive her car through the car wash. I could not believe it!

I went to the exit of the car wash and waited for the car and Bob to approach. He was surprised when he saw me. At the time, I was pregnant and showing. Bob got out of the car and ran to me. I told him that I did not like seeing him driving that lady's car with her almost on top of him. He promised that next time, he would have someone else drive her through the car wash. I believed him.

A few months later, we began preparing the nursery; I was due in March of the coming year. Bob's mom, Louise, gave me the baby crib Bob used when he was a baby and a rocking chair. The baby was growing very fast. Christmas passed, and we had big expectations for the new year.

One day after work, again I passed by the gas station, and Bob was working on some lady's car. I approached them, and I saw that she had her boobs on top of the fender, almost exposing them. When Bob saw me, he got kind of nervous and went to get a tool. At that moment, I told the lady that she was not letting my husband concentrate on his work by showing him her breasts. She stood up, fixed herself, and walked away as she told Bob to call her when the car was ready. I was not jealous; I was protecting my husband from all the surrounding sharks! My goodness, these ladies did not care that he was already married! For sure, I put them in their place.

It was our first Valentine's Day as a married couple! I was almost eight months pregnant, so we decided to celebrate it at home. Dinner time passed, and Bob was not yet home. I called the gas station, and they told me he went fishing with some friends. I could not believe he was doing this to me.

On the way back, Bob remembered it was Valentine's Day. He stopped at a pharmacy and bought me a box of chocolates. When he came in and gave me the gift, it was about nine o'clock. I took the box and threw it across the room. He began apologizing, but I was so upset that I just stayed away from him that evening. He needed to tell his friends that he was a married man now, that things were different!

Here is something about me that has really bothered me all my life. I did not have any experience in cooking since my mom—and later my grandmother—did all the cooking at home. I was always busy with schoolwork and working. After we married, Bob's mom gave me a cookbook, so I learned how to make meat loaf, scalloped potatoes, lasagna, spaghetti with meatballs, roast beef, Cuban food like picadillo (like sloppy joe), chicken fricassee, chicken with rice, etc. Bob barbecued on weekends. I thought I was doing pretty well with my cooking.

One day, Bob did not come for dinner. I was waiting for him, dinner ready. I called the gas station and was told that he was at the pizzeria with some friends. I called the pizzeria and asked for him. The girl yelled, "Bob, your wife is looking for you!" I could hear everybody laughing at him. He came to the phone, and I told him that I was worried because he did not tell me anything about being late.

When he came home later that evening, I explained to Bob that I would appreciate it if he let me know so I did not worry about him or cook. I reversed the situation and asked him, "Would you like it if I was going out with my friends without letting you know?" He got the point and never did it again. Communication is very important at the beginning of a marriage.

March began, and the baby was growing so much that my belly was huge. One day at school, when I was coming down the stairs, the principal saw me with that big belly and told me to stay home because she was afraid the baby was going to be born at school.

Two weeks after I left school, our first son, Bobby, was born. Twenty-one days later, the principal called me and begged me to come back to work because they really needed me in the learning lab. If I did not return, she was going to hire someone else to take my place. The following Monday, I went to work and left the baby with a babysitter at our home. I cried when I left him! The problem was that I was still classified as a full-time substitute; I did not have my continuing teaching contract yet, not even medical insurance. I did not want to lose my teaching job, but I felt so guilty leaving my baby!

Bob was so busy at the gas station that he was not home much either. It was very difficult for me to deal with both work and the baby. I cried almost every day! I was under a lot of pressure at work and dealing with guilt when I left the baby with the sitter. I even thought about quitting my job! Then I realized that a job like mine was very difficult to find. The principal also began giving me a hard time if I got to work five or ten minutes late; even when my planning time was the first hour of the day, she wrote me up if I was late and put it in my file. I was exhausted, physically and emotionally. My mother was working, so she could not help me.

That year, Aunt Marta moved away from the cold weather and bought a house on my parents' block. We were all very happy with her move! She found a teaching job right away and loved living finally in sunny Florida. Her son Mayito and his family lived not too far from her.

Juggling being a mother and wife, trying to be a good cook, and working full time was not easy. One day while having dinner, Bob criticized my cooking and told me that he did not want to eat my food any longer. I could not believe it; I was trying my best to be a good cook.

The following day, I called a Cuban catering service and arranged for them to deliver dinner every night. The first night, when Bob got home, I was in the den playing with the baby. He came in, kissed us, and said, "I do not smell dinner." At that moment, someone knocked on the door. He opened it and received the food containers. He asked me, "What is this?"

I said, "Dinner." I told him about what I had done. I set the table, served the food, and we enjoyed the dinner.

We did this for a week. We had different Cuban meals every night, and I enjoyed the fact that I did not have to cook. The last day, he begged me to please stop the catering service and said that he liked the way I cooked more than the catering service's food. He apologized for what he said to me, kissed me, and begged me to cook again. I stopped the service and began cooking the following week. The catered food was okay for me, but Bob wanted some American food instead of Cuban food every day. I did not understand; he had eaten Cuban food almost every day at my parents' house when we were dating. But, of course, I was not the cook. He loved my grandmother's Cuban meals!

One day, we took the baby with us to close the gas station. Bobby was playing on my lap in front of the desk. In one second, he slipped and hit his forehead, between his eyes, on the edge of the desk and cut the bridge of his nose. We had to take him to the emergency room to receive stitches. Bobby was about eight months old, and I was holding him while the doctor stitched his forehead. The doctor's hands were shaking, and this made me nervous. The baby kept crying, which made it worse. We were worried that he was going to have a scar between his eyes for life, but thank God it faded.

In 1978, I began getting ready to become an American citizen. Hours were spent studying the booklet that contained many of the questions I could be asked by a government officer when taking the citizenship test and going through the interview. It was a very exciting and proud moment and much more meaningful when on July 4, 1978, together with my husband and our son Bobby, I pledged allegiance to the flag and became a citizen of the United States of America.

I was already pregnant again with our other son, Marc, who was born in December of that year. This time, I had a continuing teaching contract and medical insurance, so we did not have to pay for the hospital. I had a baby and a twenty-one-month-old child. I was able to find someone to come to our home to take care of our babies. Less than a year later, my mother came to help me with the children for a while.

An old lady, a cus-tomer of the gas station, told Bob that her friend was moving into a condo, and she was selling her baby grand piano for $400 because it did not fit in her new place. Bob borrowed a pickup truck and brothers-in-law Roly and Frank helped him bring the piano home. It was my Valentine's Day gift in 1978! I loved it and began playing right away. Then I began composing music! Many pictures were taken in front of this

beautiful piano over the years of our marriage, like this one, where I am with our two sons.

Bob's family decided to get out of the service-station business. He was not happy with his family's decision, but what could he do? We needed to adjust to these changes at home too. Bob began doing some cooking, which made my life easier. He found a job at another service station not far from our home. He managed and hired the gas-pump-island employees and supervised and performed mechanical repairs as he was the only certified auto technician at this business. Every morning, he opened the station, but he did not have to do the closing at night anymore. Of course, it was not the same as managing his family business while sharing the mechanical work with his brothers.

Bob was a little frustrated with his new job because his idea of customer relations was different from the owner's. After all, back in 1978, Bob was recognized by his customers for exemplary service and was named Dealer of the Year in the Miami–Ft. Lauderdale region. A little while after Bob started working at his new job, he was offered a sole proprietorship of another Amoco service station. In the end, though, he could not make a satisfactory, worthwhile deal, so the deal did not go through. Sometimes, in life, things happen for a reason, and I believe this was one of them.

At the end of 1979, Grandmother Aurora—we called her Mamama—was already eighty-three years old, and she had not seen her only son since she left Cuba in 1967.

My mother was afraid she was going to die without seeing him again. They decided to visit him in Cuba. When they got to Cuba, Mamama asked Mother to make sure she was not left there. She could not take dealing again with the flies, living without air-conditioning, and sleeping under a mosquito net. She was happy to spend a week with her son, visit her brothers and sisters who were still alive, and see her nieces and nephews. Uncle Juan promised her that he would join us in the US as soon as he could. It was difficult for his two sons, Tatoño and Alberto, and their families, who were still in Cuba. Chito had left in 1967 and was enjoying freedom with his wife, Magaly, and their two children, Lizbet and Juan Carlos, who were born in Cuba, plus Danny, who was born in the US.

During the Mariel Boatlift in 1980, which is better explained in the next chapter, my father, my cousin Chito, and my brothers-in-laws Juan and Rolando chartered a vessel to go to Cuba to pick up the families they had left behind. When they got to Cuba and claimed them, the only ones who decided to leave Cuba at that time were Aunt Mirta with her husband, Miguel, their two sons, Miguel Angel and Justo, and Uncle Gonzalo. The rest of the family was afraid to leave because of all the reprisals suffered by those leaving. The Communist regime commandeered our vessel for a bunch of Cubans they had pulled out of jail; our family members were forced onto a different vessel. Bob and I had to go to Key West to pick them up a few days later. When Fidel saw the thousands of people who were leaving the country, he emptied the jails and began sending criminals among the refugees. Fidel Castro did the same with people hospitalized for tuberculosis, leprosy, and mental issues.

Our new school followed the Comprehensive Employment and Training Act (CETA) programs for out-of-school youth, dropouts, and adults studying a skill. We had students of all ages and needs in the classroom. We also offered once-a-week employability-skills classes to help our students get ready for work. Of course, most of the time, I helped the students hone their math skills. The other teacher loved this since he knew it was my strongest subject. Years later, the adult basic test was computerized and the results printed; even the study schedule was formulated by the computerized program. There was no need to write the individualized study plans anymore!

My coworker became a steward for the teachers' union, so he had to be away from the classroom a great deal. I even became a member of that union. Eventually, another teacher was assigned to work in my coworker's place since he was too busy with his new duties. The new teacher and I worked together very well and shared the duties. Of course, when there was a mathematical issue, I was the one who worked with the student. I loved this type of classroom setting, especially seeing the students progress in their knowledge and advance to new levels. The students loved it too. Many were able to pass their

GED test, which made it easier for them to find employment after learning a skill.

I was so proud of our school that I even composed the school song. Some of the students began singing it after I played it for them. That was how a choir was formed, and during special school assemblies and graduations, they sang the national anthem and the school song. One of the students had an especially beautiful voice, so I made sure she also sang at assemblies. Our school represented a step forward for its adult students. They were so proud of all their achievements, and I made sure that they knew we were too, with cards, thank-yous, etc.

As time went on, I was assigned to a new classroom. I worked in the learning lab until 1980, when the school system created the Cuban-Haitian program for all the new immigrants who were coming to school to learn English first, before they could be moved into a vocational program. I oversaw this effort, and there was a time I had forty students; they couldn't even fit in my classroom. We had to open the door, and some of the students sat in the hall.

I could not sleep at night, thinking about my classroom situation and the lack of necessary materials. It was unexpected and kind of crazy circumstances. Suddenly, we were dealing with all these students, some with formal education, others completely illiterate. I was feeling so frustrated as a teacher since I could not meet my students' educational needs. At the same time, I was working on my master's degree.

In a matter of three years, our lives really changed. We were dealing with the responsibility of two children and new life situations, but because our love was strong, we confronted the circumstances and did the best we could in providing not only material things but happiness for our children. We were thrilled with being parents. The Lord had blessed us with two healthy children, jobs, and a nice home.

Bob continued working at the gas station until one morning when the school principal asked me if Bob could teach the auto-mechanics class. Bob had a bachelor's degree plus more than six years of experience working as an auto mechanic, which made it easier for him to be certified in this field. He was also fluent in Spanish, which was a great asset. He joined me at school in 1982!

Since the students wanted me to form a choir, I asked for permission from the school principal. Of course, she agreed. We practiced during lunchtime and a little bit after school. In October, we celebrated the Hispanic Heritage month, and the choir opened the ceremony by singing the national anthem and the school song. We had made folders containing the words of these songs. One of the students provided corsages with flowers from her garden, and we all wore the same type of clothes. The group looked great.

Chapter 7

TEACHING BECAME AN IMPOSSIBLE TASK

As I told you before, the school principal transferred me to a classroom in which I began dealing with a group of about forty to forty-five Cuban and Haitian students who had arrived in Miami. In 1980, Cubans came during the Mariel Boatlift, and Haitians came in rickety vessels. They did not speak any English. It was a very difficult teaching task. My advantage was that I was able to communicate in both Spanish and French. Most of the Haitian students spoke Creole, not French. A large group of them were totally illiterate! I had to begin by teaching them the letters and their sounds. Some were able to speak French since they had received a formal education in Haiti; these students were easier to teach. Most of the Cubans were educated in their native language, but the majority did not speak any English.

I got a new babysitter, Lilia. It became difficult to wake up early in the morning to take the kids to her place. Many times, I brought the baby, Marc, still sleeping since I was able to wash only the toddler, Bobby. Thank God for Lilia; she told me to just bring the baby the way he was, and she would wash and feed him. I am a very well-organized person, and this has helped me in many ways, especially when I had so many things to do at one time.

The house was always clean. I made sure all the toys were put away at the end of the night and taught the boys to do the same. I also had a waste-basket in each room for the garbage they gener-ated. Bob and I never went to bed without doing the dishes. It was and still is a ritual!

This was the picture of Bobby's third birthday. Marc was only a year and a half. We always tried to give our children a birthday party every year, inviting their cousins and children in the neighborhood.

After all the rush at home, when I got to school, it was chaotic. All those adult students waiting for me to take care of them. Too many of them at one time, all with dif-ferent difficulties, learning levels, knowledge, etc. and unable to speak English. This craziness got to me. I can imagine how difficult must be for the teachers who are dealing today with all those immigrants coming across our open borders!

One morning that the babysitter had something to do, I had to drop the kids off at my parents' house. Driving back to school, on the street were children walking to school; just one block away from my parents' home and my job, this small five-year-old child, who was walking with a group of young kids, jumped off the sidewalk and into the path of my car. I was terrified when I saw I was going to hit him. I made a sharp left turn into someone's yard, hit a utility pole's tension cable, and broke it. I believe the tension cable hit the child.

The neighbors called 911 immediately, and he was taken to the hospital. I was so shaken that I could not stop crying. Someone took me into her house and let me use the restroom; then the police came to interrogate me. I told them what happened, that I tried to avoid hitting the child and really did not know how he got hurt.

I used the kind lady's house phone, called Bob, and told him about the accident. He came right away and took me over to my mother's. He called school for me and told the principal what happened and that I could not go to work. She then informed Bob that it was the son of one of my students. Bob did not know how to break the news to me. He knew this was going to make me feel worse. Bob took the kids and me home, and his brother drove my car to the gas station. He stayed with us since he needed to tell me what happened to this child. Finally, he told me the child died. I was so devastated that I could not even go to work and face that student and his classmates.

Some of my students sent their pastor to comfort me, trying to convince me that it was not my fault. The priest at our church also helped me during that time of so much pain and sorrow. I looked at our children, then thought about that poor child who lost his life and how horrible it must be for his parents and other siblings who witnessed the accident. Then I wondered, *Why wasn't an adult walking that small child to school?* I became very overprotective of my children after this awful experience.

After almost a month away from work, the principal called me and told me that I needed to return to work. She reminded me that she would have to give my job to someone else since she needed someone at school right away to deal with all those students. I thought work would help keep my mind off the accident. Also, I was working with a lawyer because the child's family sued me.

It was not easy at all to work with all these students without an aide or enough materials. I could barely sleep at night, thinking about the accident and facing the following day. I kept telling myself that I needed to be strong and face reality. I could not change what happened, and I must deal with the actual situation. Working with all these students from different backgrounds, languages, customs, etc. was a lot of pressure. You could hear them speaking their native languages among themselves. I had to make it a rule that only English could be spoken in the classroom; that way, I hoped this would maintain discipline and the idle talk to a minimum.

I loved the morning school-opening ritual of the Pledge of Allegiance, the national anthem, and the moment of silent meditation. I had to explain to the students in Spanish and French what it was. I translated both the Pledge of Allegiance and the national anthem into both languages and made a copy for each student, one side in English and the other one in their language. They read along as it was played.

One day, one of the students began singing the Cuban national anthem too. Then, the following day, the Haitian students began singing the Haitian national anthem. I wrote both down and gave them to the students, so we sang all of them first thing in the morning. I still remember the Haitian one, and, of course, I know the Cuban national anthem by heart.

The next thing I had to do was group the students according to their knowledge. We did not have a test for that at the time. The ones who never had formal education were grouped differently and worked with audiovisual cards to learn the sounds of the letters and numbers, then practice writing them. The middle group of students and the most advanced were able to work with sentences using a higher-level audiovisual card program and cassettes for reading. While one group worked with the cards, I worked with another group, moving from one group to another one to keep them busy learning.

Using the board, I taught the basic English verbs to the advanced group and then gave them an assignment that applied the lesson just taught. After that, I moved to the other group, and we worked with reading, language, or math, whichever was needed. During planning time, I prepared the handouts they needed to complete after their lessons. The students stayed with me the entire day. At the end of the school day, I was exhausted.

After months of dealing with this situation, the principal decided that the most advanced students should attend the adult basic-education reading class. This really made it easier for the students and me since I had more time to dedicate to the rest of the class.

Let me tell you what created this massive Cuban migration. On April 1, 1980, several Cubans got on a bus and drove through the fence of the Peruvian embassy in Havana. After they were granted political asylum, Fidel Castro retaliated against the Peruvian government by having the Cuban guards removed from the embassy. What Fidel did not expect was that more than 10,000 people would cram onto the embassy's grounds; some even climbed the trees since there was no space left on which to stand. Everyone wanted to leave the dictatorship!

Under these circumstances, Fidel decided to open the port of Mariel for anyone who wished to leave the country, to do so, if they had someone to pick them up. More than 125,000 Cubans fled, and this overwhelmed the Florida coast. This made Castro look bad; therefore, he put jailed common criminals and mental patients on the departing boats as well. In October of the same year, the USA stopped this migration. In addition to the Cubans, some 25,000 Haitians entered the USA during this time. Then, President Jimmy Carter declared a state of emergency and established the Cuban-Haitian Entrant Program, which offered assistance in settling in the USA.

Too many students in the classroom!! I had to open the classroom door and put some desks in the hall. Also, some students began complaining about the body odors of those students who did not bathe regularly or wear deodorants. During my planning time, I went to see the school counselor and explained the situation. She couldn't do anything about the space problem, but she was able to get some hygiene kits.

I prepared a lesson about cleanliness. I showed the students what each thing in the hygiene kit was and how to use it. I gave each student a kit, which contained toothpaste, toothbrush, comb, soap, and deodorant. They were happy to receive them. The situation got better, but still some of the guys came to school in the same smelly shirts. Then I told them that they needed to wash their clothes because, even though they wore deodorant, their dirty, smelly shirts defeated the purpose. Well, the lesson was learned, and everybody smelled nice after that.

Among the Cuban students I had in my class, one of them acted very aggressively, as if something was mentally wrong with him. He always caused problems with the Haitian students, calling them names and trying to start fights. He told me right to my face that he hated me because I came to the USA before the boatlift and that he did not want to be in my classroom. Unfortunately, I could not transfer him to another class because he did not know any English.

One morning, this student began arguing with another student in front of the classroom door. I called the school's new counselor, who was Haitian and knew Spanish too, to see what was happening outside the door. I went outside to check too. While I was talking to the combative student, right in front of the counselor, he began threatening me. He told me that he was going to put a bomb under my car, that he was going to blow me to pieces, and that he did not care if he was sent to jail since he already had been in one. By translating his tirade into English, I made sure the counselor knew what he was saying. The counselor took the student to his office. He never came back to my classroom, but I was still worried that he would go through with his threat.

I continued working well with the rest of the students since the problem student was out of the picture. Still, every time I left school, I was nervous as I started my car while wondering if this guy could have gone through with his threat and put a bomb under my car. Just in case, I carried with me all his personal information, including his address. Since he lived near our home, I always looked around and used caution when starting my car. We did not have a garage, so the car was always parked outside. I tried to continue my life in peace and not to think about it.

During the '79–'80 school year, Florida International University (FIU) was offering a master of science degree in diagnostic teaching, and there were scholarships for teachers like me, those who were dealing with adults suffering from different learning disabilities and other mental issues. Several of my teacher friends—for example, Mercy, who lived in my neighborhood—and I decided to enroll in this program. We applied, and each of us was given one of these scholarships. All these courses were offered at night. Mercy and I took advantage of it and graduated in August 1981. My field of focus was emotional disturbance.

Several days a week, after I got home from work after picking up the kids, I cooked dinner, ate something, and went to school. Thank God that Bob helped me by taking care of the kids while I was at school. It was not easy for me since I had to cook, feed the kids, and leave for FIU.

My goal was to learn about how to deal in my classroom with students who were suffering from many mental issues and learning disabilities. I met nice people while taking these courses. One of the courses was psychology, which was taught by a Cuban psychologist. He was a nicely dressed, middle-aged man. He asked me if I was Cuban; of course, my answer was yes. I told him about the three years I had to suffer in forced-labor camps just because my family presented documentation to leave the country. That was the only conversation I had with him. He was never too friendly after that.

Later, in 2006, we heard on the news that this nice professor, Carlos, and his wife, Elsa, who also worked in Counseling and Psychological Services at FIU, were accused of spying for Cuba. I could not believe what I was hearing, but when I saw their pictures on the news, I knew who they were. It was a shock! You never know with whom you are dealing and what their mentality is.

Many times, I wonder about the kind of information they were gathering for Cuba. They were part of the Cuban community, a married couple with children. Who would think they were spies? I also worried about how many of the young students had professors like them, with the same beliefs, indoctrinating them into the Marxist ideology? This is what has been happening to our youth in high school and college. They are dealing with teachers who promote Socialist/Communist agendas. This is very worrisome for me since I have lived it; I know this monster.

We decided to send Bobby to the nursery school at the neighborhood church. He cried when I left him there the first morning, but got used to it right away. He adjusted to the ambience and made some friends. It benefited him socially and intellectually. So, thereafter, Marc was the only child I had to take to the babysitter.

Let me tell you about something funny that happened in the classroom; I will never forget it. I was teaching a group of Haitians and Cubans different words, their sounds, and their meanings. One of them was *explosive*. There was a Cuban student who was kind of mentally challenged. He was such a nice gentleman, very well-mannered, and his name was Antonio. I was showing the word card, but some of the Haitian students did not understand its meaning. Antonio stood up, waved his arms, and made an explosion sound with his mouth. We all laughed so much just watching his demonstration.

Another funny thing occurred when I was trying to teach the word *"knock."* I began singing Paul McCartney's "Let 'Em In." I knocked on the classroom's door and simulated the sound of a doorbell. At this moment, Antonio got up, left the classroom, and began knocking at the door. I opened it, and he said, "Good morning!" We all laughed. He was so much fun to have around. I never forgot him.

I used a lot of drawings and pictures on the board to help the students understand. Many nights, when I got home, I cut pictures of things from magazines and pasted them on a paper so the students could visually see what I was trying to convey. We did not have the necessary materials to teach such a large group of immigrants.

A new janitor, Amable, began working at the school, and he was the one who cleaned my classroom. What a great job he always did! He was Cuban, but a descendant of Spaniards from the Canary Islands, like my maternal grandparents. He knew about all kinds of cures in the form of teas made from different plants. If I had a headache, he brought me a tea to ease my pain. He was the best janitor the school had. He kept the floors shiny and the school clean. He also maintained the plants around the building. After a while, he became a good friend, and still today, we keep in touch. Unfortunately, his wife died in her sixties from breast cancer.

Going back to the classroom, when a student's functional level improved, they were transferred to a vocational class of their own choosing. Some of these students were able to read English, but still had trouble conversing in it. The English lessons were geared to teach them the necessary vocabulary for their selected vocational area. Each day, they continued spending an hour in the learning lab to improve their reading, math, and language skills.

In February 1981, I received a Certificate of Recognition for Outstanding Service to Vocational Education, which was given by the school principal. At the second annual Vocational Training Awards presentation, which took place in May of the same year, for the first time our choir sang the school song that I composed. We sang with orchestration I had recorded by a musician I knew, Nestor. In August of the same year, I graduated from Florida International University with a master's degree in diagnostic teaching with a major in emotional disturbance, which helped me better understand some of my students.

As I mentioned before, I had a great babysitter who became my friend. One Saturday that Lilia and I went shopping with the kids, an incident happened that I have never forgotten. We went to the Cutler Ridge Mall and were trying on some clothes at a small store next to JCPenney. I left the kids with her when I went to change. Marc was in his stroller—the one that you can carry like an umbrella— since he was a few months past his second birthday. Bobby was four years old then and already acting like an older kid.

When I came out of the changing room, which was right next to where they were, I asked her where Bobby was. She thought he went into the changing room with me. I dropped the clothes, ran outside, and saw Bobby at the other end of the mall, where the Sears store was. I began running towards him, yelling his name. He kept walking and could not hear me. Finally, I reached him and embraced him. We were both crying! I told him not stray from us ever again. Lilia, also crying, approached with Marc. What a frightening moment! It is unbelievable how things can happen in an instant.

A year later, Lilia was diagnosed with breast cancer. She went through surgery followed by chemotherapy. It was devastating news because she was more than my baby-sitter; she was my friend. One early morning while I was getting ready for work, I received a call from the hospital. It was Lilia! She called to tell me how much she appreciated my friendship; she felt she was burning out, like a candle, and did not know if she would see me again. She needed to tell me how much she loved me. She was only fifty-five! It was a very sad time for me too; I lost a close friend.

We hired one of the neighbors to babysit for Marc at my home. One morning, my mother went to my house to check on things, and through the window, she saw the sitter feeding the baby while he was lying on the kitchen countertop; his highchair sat empty next to him. My mom could not believe it. She had a key to the house, so she entered and told the sitter not to do that, but to feed the baby in his highchair. No wonder Marc was having some breathing problems!

We were so proud of our cute boys. We had an intercom in their bedrooms so we could hear them at night when we were in our master bedroom, on the other side of the house. I began noticing that Marc's breathing was not regular. He stopped breathing for a little while; then I heard him gasping for breath. We took him to a Dr. Santiago Hernandez, whose aunt, Dr. Irene Hernandez, a pharmacist, was married to my father's first cousin, Joaquin

Barnet, a lawyer in Matanzas. We had known each other since we were children.

After we explained to him about Marc's breathing, and he checked Marc, he told us that Marc was suffering from sleep apnea, that he needed to have his adenoids and tonsils out to alleviate this problem. He was just two years old when he had this surgery. We both cried when he was taken into surgery while still so little. When he woke up, you should have seen the mad look on his face. He was in pain, and he thought it was our fault. Poor baby. Thank God my mother was great at helping me at home with Marc after surgery.

Looking back, I can see that I had too much going on during the years 1980 and 1981. No wonder I was so tense and exhausted while trying to deal with children, work, and finishing a degree. Finally, in 1982, the school principal assigned a teacher's aide to work with me. She was able to speak Spanish and English, which was an advantage. It was easier for me to teach and help the students in a more individualized way. She was a very pleasant lady, and we got along very well. The students were glad that we were able to give them the much-needed additional attention and help.

In 1982, Commissioner Demetrio Perez, Jr. presented me with a certificate of recognition for my exemplary work and dedication to my students and for elevating my education to new levels. I really appreciated his recognition even though I did not feel special for doing my job.

Many of my students left school and began working since they needed to support their families. I believe, by then, they were no longer receiving government stipends. Someone needed to work! The group got smaller, and it was easier to work with them. What a difference it made having a teacher's aide too! Now I could work individually with my students. I did not use a board anymore. I wrote notes in their notebooks so they could review and practice at home later.

Chapter 8

THINGS CAN GET COMPLICATED SOMETIMES

In 1982, Bob was hired to be the auto-mechanics instructor. He loved the school and the fact that he had a beautiful shop with a nice classroom. He had already taken some education courses in college, so he went through teacher training on Saturdays to receive his teaching certification for the state of Florida.

Later, he also went to school at night to receive cultural-language training in Haitian Creole. He learned all the necessary vocabulary to deal with his Haitian students. Since Bob was fluent in Spanish, this helped him as well with his Spanish-speaking students. He was ready to do the job and happy he was able to help these adults learn a vocation that would benefit them in the future.

The shop was outfitted with the necessary tools and equipment to teach automotive technology. The class had a mixture of American and foreign students—some with different levels of skill while many with little to no skill, but eager to learn. Since the program was open-entry, open-exit, the teaching necessitated individualized instruction and competency-based learning. Bob enjoyed producing instructional materials that he incorporated into his lesson plans to facilitate the learning process.

Bob and I shared ideas about how to deliver the lessons in a way that helped the students achieve their objectives in this nontraditional learning environment. In addition, we loved working together, especially having the same lunchtime. We shared our teaching experiences. I was still teaching English, but it was much easier having a manageable number of students plus someone to give me a helping hand.

Our children began attending the Montessori School, which was in the farming area called Redland. Marc met a new friend there, Gan. His father was a doctor at the local hospital. He was a widower who lived with his mother and sister. If he was in surgery, he asked us take his son to our home, and he picked him up there later. Many times, when that happened, they both stayed over for dinner. We became close friends; even today, we are still in contact. We feel they are a part of our family.

The Montessori educational system is an individualized, self-directed approach to learning in which children show their creativity. It helped our sons develop their abilities and intellect. It was much better for them to be in this type of environment during the summer than a day-care center or at home with a babysitter. It was expensive, but worth it. They were surrounded by plenty of materials and were even singing French songs while playing an instrument. They also made many friends and were invited to many birthday parties. We were glad we took this step with their education.

The following year, Bobby's Montessori School teacher wanted him to stay another year in kindergarten because she thought he was not mature enough to advance a grade. I assured her that Bobby was bored in her class, that he did not need to repeat it, but that he needed more challenging materials. Well, she kept him in her classroom, and he was very bored repeating the same books. The following year, he began first grade.

In 1984, we decided to send the kids to our local public school, Avocado Elementary. It was easier for us since we did not have to drive that far to take the kids to school. Bobby began second grade and Marc first grade. Immediately, his teacher noticed that Bobby was too advanced for her class and asked us to have him tested. We did and found out that Bobby was gifted. That teacher who told us that

Bobby was immature was wrong! He was placed in a special combined program; he spent some days in a gifted program and others in his regular class. Marc was also tested, and he was just a few points from also being classified as gifted; we were told that he has a photographic memory.

Going back to our own school, Bob and I got along very well with the school staff and teachers. As a matter of fact, all the teachers and staff worked together in harmony for the best of the school, but the principal did not like this. She told her staff that they needed to stay away from the teachers so that they could do a better job. I could not believe she was acting this way. The school registrar, Carmen, had been my neighbor since I was single and moved to the first house I purchased with my parents in Leisure City. She even came to our wedding! We were like family, but, now, we were expected to act like strangers at work.

Then teachers were not allowed to enter the main office! The principal moved the sign-in book and the cabinet with all the classroom keys to the back room. Before, this cabinet was in the middle of the main office, next to the principal's office, so you walked through the office saying hi to everybody. Because of this change, you had to enter the back door to the small back room, where all the cables for computers and phones were, across from the bathrooms, at the beginning of the hall, almost in front of the lunchroom. At the end of the hall was the conference room. It was okay with me, so we did not have to face the principal every morning.

If you needed something from one of the staff members, you had to go to the office's main entrance and ask for the person you needed to speak to. Well, things were different, and this was creating animosity among the instructional personnel and the staff. We teachers were seen as enemies! Anyways, I always tried to avoid the office, especially when the principal was there, and we knew when she was there because she wore a very pungent perfume that you could smell from long distances, and it permeated the main office. It was too strong for my taste. I really don't know how the office staff could stand that scent!

That school principal wanted total control of her staff. She did not want to have any interference from the teachers. She had a totalitarian way of controlling her office staff and wanted to separate them from the teachers, who did not like her controlling style. She did not want the teachers to see her weaknesses, so she hid behind her staff for support.

By this time, I was trying to publish a Spanish book of poetry, *Algo de Mi*, which in English means *Something from Me*. Most of the poems were written while I was still in Cuba; I had kept them for years in two notebooks. Aunt Mirta brought them from Cuba when she left in 1980. She also brought some pictures but could not bring anything else. The government did not give her any time to take anything out of her house when they came for her family and her during the Mariel Boatlift.

My father was reluctant for me to publish it. When I wrote these poems in Cuba and read them to him, he thought that they were too passionate for a girl my age and did not want me to show them to anybody; he was worried about what people would think of me. I assured him that they were just part of my imagination, nothing to worry about it.

I told Bob about it, and he encouraged me to put them all together in a book and publish it, which meant typing them and sending them off. In those years, it was more difficult to be published. Well, I was very glad he pushed me to do it, and in 1983 the book was done. Later, I was recognized by the Cuban Teachers Association, to which I belonged, for the publishing of my book.

In February 1983, I received a letter from the assistant superintendent, congratulating me on being selected by my coworkers as our school's Teacher of the Year. I had to write my teaching philosophy. In this letter, the assistant superintendent expressed that he was happy to see how highly I was regarded by the staff, and he was sure my students felt the same way. Then in March of the same year, I was invited to the Teacher of the Year Luncheon sponsored by the Greater Miami Chamber of Commerce. I really did not care much for recognition since I always tried to do my job well. I was happier when the students thanked me for their success, rather than my own.

In 1984, I was a state finalist for Teacher of the Year and received an award certificate from the school department during a luncheon. Among all the finalists, one was selected as the state winner. I was glad I received the school's recognition after so much work during those previous years. My coworkers believed that I really deserved it. Thank you from the bottom of my heart! In August, I was also recognized by the Cuban Teachers in Exile Association for all my achievements.

In 1985, we purchased a small farm, one and a half acres, in an area called Redland. The house was not that big, but big enough for us. It had three small bedrooms and two bathrooms, and the kitchen was very small. It also had a small formal living room and a small family room. The garage was huge! We decided to take half of this huge garage, move the kitchen there, and build a porch along the back of the family room and kitchen. After remodeling it, the kitchen was big, as was the dining room, and they both had windows facing the land. We spent thousands of dollars remodeling this old place, but still, for whatever reason, I did not feel happy there. The bedrooms, closets, and bathrooms were too small for my taste. It was not our dream home. I kept looking for a bigger place without telling Bob. On Sundays, while he was watching a game on television, I took the kids with me for a ride around Redland, the farming area south of Miami.

I saw in the *South Dade News Leader* a sales ad for Great Dane puppies. I was not familiar with this type of dog. After school, I went to see them. As I arrived at this farm, a huge dog greeted me. Its head was up to the top of my car window. I was afraid to get out of the car, but the dog's owner assured me that it was okay. I got out, and she took me to the garage where, in a box, she had some puppies. She told me that because of her size, when the Great Dane had lain down to feed her puppies, one of them got under her, and it was suffocated. When I saw a white puppy with blue eyes and dark spots, I fell in love. It was a harlequin. The lady told me that the puppies were only twenty-one days old. I thought they were too young to be taken from their mother, but the woman said that it was okay.

When Bob got home and saw the puppy, he could not believe I just went out and bought it without asking him. As soon as I told him that the puppy's eyes reminded me of his, it was okay with him. That night, the puppy would not stop crying. I had to go to the garage, get him out of the box, and rock him to sleep. I fed him like a baby, with a bottle. He loved to be cuddled, and the kids were thrilled to have him. He really grew fast, as you can see from the picture!

One day that we had workers remodeling the house, the puppy got into my closet and took my brand-new pair of leather boots to the yard. He destroyed them! When I looked outside and saw him doing that, I screamed at him, but the damage was already done. I had to throw my boots away. To the kids, this was so funny.

Finally, I began having some normalcy in my classroom. The students had assimilated more into the American culture, and it was easier to deal with them. My classroom was not as crowded as it had been, so I was able to work on the students' weak areas. My life had also settled, and the kids were going to the Montessori School during the summer. Bob and I rode together to work and took the kids to their school on the way. We had time to enjoy our family and do more things together.

At the beginning of this school year, our sons were able to enter Sacred Heart School. Bobby began third grade and

Marc second. Some days, Bobby continued attending the gifted classes at the public school. We were so happy that the boys were finally accepted into the Catholic private school. Bob and I had attended Catholic schools all our lives, and we wanted the same for our children.

This happiness did not last long. Almost at the end of the year, the school principal told Bob that she needed him to work the night shift! As soon we got home from work, after picking up the kids from school, I had to cook right away and have dinner ready before Bob had to go back to work at 5:30 p.m. His night-shift schedule was from 6:00 p.m. to 10:00 p.m. Of course, the kids missed their father. By the time Bob returned home, they were sleeping, and mornings were total chaos. We had to be at school at 8:00 a.m., and our planning time was during the school hours. We, and sometimes just I, woke up every morning at 5:00 a.m. to get the kids ready, take them to school, and, from there, rush back to our school.

One morning when I got to work, I was called to the principal's office, and she informed that she no longer had a position for me at our school. She was going to recommend that I be assigned to another vocational school, perhaps in Miami. That day was to be my last one. I could not believe it! But I was not totally surprised because I had noticed that the principal had been intentionally ignoring or bypassing me about school matters. There was another teacher, Ms. P., who was hired a few months prior to my being classified as surplus. Why did she get hired if there were too many teachers?

When I went to my classroom, I informed the students that it was my last day, that I was going to be transferred to another school because there was not teaching position available for me at this center. By lunchtime, the word that it was my last day had gotten around. Students began protesting on the sidewalk and in the parking lot in front of the building; they did not go to class. One of them went into the migrant-workers' office to call the news media to report what the principal was doing to me.

Immediately, the executive secretary working at the migrants' office ran into the school office and told the school principal what the students were going to do. The principal then went outside, begged the students to come back to class, and said that it was a misunderstanding. The students replied that they did not want me to leave, that I was a great, dedicated teacher. As soon as the principal went back to her office, she called me in and told me to forget about that letter, that she was not going to transfer me, and to please tell the students to go back to class. I walked outside and told the students that I was staying. They began clapping and happily went back to class. What was wrong with her? Did she have a teacher friend in mind to take over my position? Unbelievable!

After that, the relationship between the principal and me got worse. The union steward was always lurking around, and I felt as if she was watching me. So I began watching them back and writing down everything I saw wrong. I went everywhere with a yellow pad, writing things down.

One morning, the school principal called me to her office. This time, she was sweet, trying to find out what I was doing going around the school with a yellow pad. I told her that I was just writing down whatever I thought was wrong. She tried to convince me that she was my friend, that she would not do anything to hurt me. My simple answer was okay, and I left. I did not trust her anymore.

Poor Bob was exhausted, and weekends were busy too! On Saturdays, I cleaned the house and did the laundry while Bob took care of the yard. The kids were also busy running around the yard or playing on the back porch. Sundays were more relaxing; there was always something going on, like the birthday party of one of the friends' kids or someone in our large family. My mother was always available to listen to our problems and help us find a solution. We could also count on my father, who always had an intelligent opinion. It was a blessing to have parents whom you could trust and listen to what they had to say. Anyways, they had more experience than we did, plus they loved us and wished us the best in life.

Looking back at those years, thank God we were young and had the energy to deal with our busy lives. We worked during the entire year, except for three weeks in August that were not paid. We always planned something for the school breaks—traveling to different states and countries or simply enjoying the nearby beach. The trips during Christmas vacations or spring breaks were great, but we always were home in time to celebrate it with family. Our sons were doing great in school, and both were in good health; that was very important to us.

We needed to get away from work and enjoy life with our children. We looked for places to reinforce their learning experiences, such as visiting museums, St. Augustine, Toronto in Canada, and Cancun in Mexico, where we bought a time-share because we could transfer it to different places.

Three of my students from the Dominican Republic, who were already studying air-conditioning in the morning, and ESOL and ABE in the afternoon, told me that there was a "teacher" working in the child-care department; every time they went to the restroom, he came after them and began making nasty gestures and seemed to be asking them for sex. They reported him to their ESOL teacher, who got very upset with their accusations. These students became angry with the ESOL teacher and told me that they were going to beat up the child-care guy if he accosted them again while they were using the restroom. I tried to calm them down and told them to just watch out for each other, not to cause any trouble that could affect their status in this country. They listened to me and decided not to attend the ESOL classes anymore to avoid any conflict with the teacher.

A few weeks later, the ESOL teacher died in a car accident. He was seventy-six years old. The principal was very upset about his loss since they were very close friends. Some of the students told me that, one Sunday, they saw them both holding a headless chicken and dripping its blood on the ground around the school, apparently practicing voodoo. When the principal heard he had passed away, she began crying and yelling in the school hall, "They killed him!" She was referring to those Dominican students. She believed they did some voodoo to the ESOL teacher and caused him to die. To me, all of that was ignorance. After that, these students left the school for good.

One day during my planning time, I stopped by the child-care class. It had a glass window to the hall, so anybody could look inside and see the students taking care of the infants. This day, I saw the male teacher's aide, the one who was spying on the Dominican students in the bathroom, sticking his tongue into the mouth of a baby and letting it suck on it. I could not believe my eyes! I thought about what I would do if that were my baby and someone was doing that to him. I went to the office and talked to the counselor. She told me to write a report so she could present it to the principal.

The principal called the school counselor and me to her office. She wanted me to tell her what happened. I told her, and I also informed her that as a teacher, I had to report anything I thought was wrong. Her reply was that I should have told her first, instead of writing a report and giving it to the counselor. My response was that I was following the rules. The child-care teacher's aide was removed from our school, but not prosecuted; he was sent to a place that housed disabled adults. I could not believe it! The school had students from that facility too.

As a matter of fact, I had two guys from that facility in my class the entire day. One of them, Heb, was very sweet and always telling me how much he missed his mother and going to church with her. His mother had passed away a few years back. The other one, Ron, was more independent and mischievous. One afternoon, at almost break time, Ron, holding an apple, asked my permission to go to the restroom. He signaled Heb and left; Heb followed him. A few minutes later, a male teacher came into my classroom to inform me what these two students seemed to be doing in the bathroom. When they came back, Heb was holding the apple. I told them, next time, they were not supposed to go together to the restroom, especially almost at break time. Heb approached my desk and apologized for the sin he had committed. I told him I did not want to hear about it, but I was glad he was sorry.

Another thing that happened one day was a problem with one of Bob's students committing a crime. The police came to investigate, to see if it was true that the student was not in class when the crime was committed. Bob showed them his attendance record for that day, and the student was there on time for class. If he committed a crime, it was done before class time.

Bob had students who were in a special program, receiving five hours of instruction in the afternoon, from 2:30 p.m. to 8:00 p.m. with a half an hour lunch break at 5:30 p.m. One of the investigators came to see Bob and showed him a copy of his own roll book that documented the weekly attendance for these ten high school students who were paid hourly. These records were given to the investigator by office personnel; it showed that each of these students was present all five hours of class. Bob also had students sign in and out in a special attendance time sheet that he kept in his classroom.

As soon as Bob looked at the attendance record with his signature at the bottom, he realized those were not the hours he reported to the office. He always kept a copy of the roll book he sent to the office, and it showed different numbers. Bob could not believe what he was seeing! He also showed the classroom-attendance record with the students' signatures he kept in his classroom. He told the officers that the records they had were not his; someone had changed the numbers. It seems that someone in the office was changing the hours the teachers were reporting, giving the students the same number of hours every day. The officers left with the proof that falsification of records had been committed, something which is penalized by law since the school was partially funded with federal money.

Things continued to go bad for this principal. One day, the school police came over again because of complaints of falsification of documents. Teachers were informed of this, so we needed to be ready when we were called. The officers began calling teachers one by one to be interviewed, since there were accusations that the teachers were falsifying the records. Students were paid to go to school, and teachers were responsible for the hours they reported to the office. Teachers always kept a copy of the attendance with the hours they reported to the school office. All the teachers had this proof, so they did not have any problems reporting the real hours the students were there.

When I went to the meeting, I was carrying the yellow pad with me since I was not sure what was going to happen. They asked me about what I was holding. I told them that it was an anecdotal record of school activities. They asked me to let them see my notes, and I did. They copied what I had written down and gave me the pad back. That was the end of all this mess. It seems that, somehow, the accusation of falsification of records was not proved.

Bob continued going to Florida International University on Saturdays during the year 1987, and he received his diploma in bilingual vocational instruction from the School of Education. He also received a Certificate of Merit in Automotive Curriculum from the University of South Florida. Those were years of a lot of pressure at work and school to achieve our goals in life plus take care of our two sons.

By that time, I was composing music and using some of the words from my poems. My mother was also composing, music and we surely enjoyed doing this together. One of my parents' neighbors told us about his son. He had graduated from high school, where he learned how to play different instruments. He did all the musical arrangements for our musical compositions, charging $100 per song. We began then to participate in different local musical festivals.

Thank God my husband was very supportive, but my father was not. He did not like the artistic ambiance and was afraid my mother and I would be corrupted by it. You could not change the way he thought, and perhaps he was right in some respect, but not in this case.

I must tell you about another coworker, Mrs. P. She taught one of the sections of the adult basic-education program and completed our team. It was her first time dealing with a program like ours—open-entry, open-exit, multileveled classes. Mrs. B and I guided her and helped her with her curriculum. I showed her how to write the students' individualized programs based on their entry exam.

We could tell that something was wrong with her health. She told me that she was a diabetic. The school principal disliked her because she had been transferred to our school from another one, so the principal began giving Mrs. P. a hard time. She even wanted us to report to her anything that Mrs. P. did wrong. One morning, Mrs. P. came to school, I noticed she was walking very slowly. After lunch, when I was returning to my classroom, I saw her sitting on the bench by the school office's entry and leaning against a tall wooden planter. I called the office right away. The paramedics came and began trying to resuscitate her. Unfortunately, she had passed away. She was still a young woman, and we were devastated by her loss.

Chapter 9

A CHANGE WAS NEEDED

By 1988, the rest of my sisters decided to move to Miami, in a neighborhood called Kendall, following the ones who had already left. They wanted their kids to attend better schools. They all purchased houses very close to each other. Years before, our parents had purchased a bigger house in the same Leisure City neighborhood where we all lived at the time. My father began working from 2:00 p.m. to 10:00 p.m. as a custodian at a school only half a block from their house. He had already been working at my husband's family's gas station from 6:00 a.m. to 1:00 p.m., and he continued to do so. He was always a hardworking person and a provider.

This new house had four bedrooms; two of them were large and had walk-in closets and bathrooms. It was much better for our grandmother who had a nice room with a window to the street, just the way she liked it. She did not have to share the bathroom with my parents. One of the bedrooms was converted into a den to watch television. After my sisters moved, I was the only daughter living close to my parents. My house was about fifteen minutes away from my parents, but they missed having the rest of the girls' families nearby.

A friend of mine who was working at the migrant office, Maria, invited me to join a club, the Homestead Civitan Club; she was its president. I was so glad she invited me to be part of this great service organization: Civitan International. Why did I join? First, because I was asked by a friend; second, because it is an organization of clubs dedicated to helping the community with an emphasis on those suffering from intellectual and developmental disabilities. The uniqueness of this organization is its Civitan International Research Center, which is dedicated to finding the cause, cure, and better treatments of many brain disorders like autism, Alzheimer's, Down and Rett syndromes, and many others.

The meetings were twice a month at a restaurant. When I got home from work, I prepared dinner for Bob and the kids, then went to the meetings. I felt that my participation in many of their projects was for the benefit of the community in which we lived. It was important for me to make a difference by paying forward to those in need. I always asked neighbors and friends to join us, so they knew we wanted them to be part of the team.

My romantic side is very vibrant, and I began composing Spanish songs, as did my mom. But my songs were ballads, and my mother's were mainly salsas. We loved having music in common and sharing moments talking about it and planning the musical arrangements done by Nestor. I used some of my poems for the lyrics of my songs.

We began participating in different musical competitions, like the Association of Critics and Commentators of Art (ACCA), which was made up of Spanish artists. The first time we participated, the song I presented received second place, and my mother's took third. I also participated in the Galaxy of Stars in Miami and was recognized with a trophy. The following year, 1989, my mother and I participated in the ACCA musical competition again. She received the first-place trophy, and I won second place. It was the first time a mother and daughter won the top honors! She was so proud, and I was very happy for her.

During that time, I also participated in the Festival OTI of Miami. I composed a song called "Quisiera Paz" ("I Want Peace"), which became one of the eight finalists. It was kind of expensive since I had to pay, first, for the musical arrangement to send to the judges, and after selection, the musical arrangement of each instrument of the orchestra. However, I felt it was worth it. My family was very happy that at least my song was selected as one of the finalists. The final competition was televised, and each of us, the participating composers, was part of the choreography. It was a beautiful musical program, and I was glad I was able to be part of it.

My mother and I also participated in other festivals like Festival Canción al Amor in Miami, where my sister

Mirtica sang one of my compositions, *"Vísteme."* There were other festivals attended by very well-known actors and actresses too. It was a fun time for all of us. Here we are after the mentioned festival.

At school, things continued being kind of shaky until one day the principal was informed that she had been transferred to a vocational center in Miami. In 1989, a new principal, Mr. T., was assigned to our center. We were all so glad to have someone new coming. This principal was completely different from the one we had before. He knew how to use the budget, and all the teachers' programs benefitted from this. I received new computers, and all the adult basic-education teachers were instructed on how to use the new and improved computerized Plato system, which I loved.

Students had the opportunity to use this computer program to work on their weak areas of reading, math, and language. Even though my area of expertise was math, those who were more advanced in this subject could work on their English or language area according to their placement tests' results. Since the instruction was individualized, I had to move from one student to the other to help them in the area they were studying. The language and reading teachers did not have this program in their classrooms; they used the individualized educational system, a personalized study schedule, based on the adult basic-education tests' results, to help their students.

During this school year, while I was taking my teacher's planning time, I prepared a group of the Spanish-speaking students to take the general equivalency diploma (GED) test in Spanish, and they successfully passed it. These students already had formal education in their countries, and it was easier for them to concentrate on learning to speak English fluently, instead of working in the adult-education program. The same thing was true of some of the Haitian students who already had formal education.

The great satisfaction was when I was invited to attend their college or university's graduations. They felt that

153

I was their motivator, someone who helped them to continue studying and become the best that they could be. It made me very happy to know all my sleepless nights were worthwhile. I was very proud of their achievements! They were so thankful that they presented me a plaque in recognition of my dedication to their successes. I have never forgotten them all these years and hope they still remember me.

In August 1989, we purchased a new home on five acres in Redland, a farming area between Miami and Homestead. Bob and I were very happy because we had fulfilled our dreams: Bob wanted a place with a lot of land, and I wanted a big house. The house had been abandoned for several years and needed a lot of work. Bob began cleaning the land while I oversaw the inside. The master bedroom's bathroom was not finished, so we had to hire someone to come and finish it. We did not like the wallpaper that was in all the rooms. Bob and I stripped it and then painted the entire interior of this 6,090-square-foot home. Our Great Dane was in his glory. He had a place to run and fruit trees to keep him full. Then we got horses, and our kids surely loved living there too.

A member of the club and I were invited to be part of the Tropical District of Civitan International. We went to the training and were surprised to see the age of some of the ones volunteering as members of the board of directors. The secretary was ninety years old! During the break, we went to the restroom, and my friend was kind of disenchanted to see that most of the people were a lot older than we were, and she thought about withdrawing. My answer to her was that if all those people were still active—and their brains were functioning remarkably at their age—it meant that by doing volunteer work you kept yourself young. She liked that and kept volunteering at the club level, but I took a position at the district level.

Bob and I were very active in all the school's extracurricular activities. Some of the ones we organized many times were the celebrations of Hispanic Heritage Month in October and Black History Month in February. We made our students participate too by drawing decorations, their countries' flags, etc. The school's new principal knew that he could count on our support and participation in these celebrations, and we loved being useful and lending a helping hand where it was needed. Most of the teachers were happy with the new principal and willing to pitch in too.

One of the activities during the Hispanic Heritage Month was the display of the flags; the students marched carrying the flags of their countries. By doing this, other students became aware of their nationalities and the flags of their native countries. We reinforced in our classrooms the customs and cultures of different countries; as you can see in the picture below, the members of the choir dressed in their indigenous attire. It was a true learning experience for them. There was folkloric dancing, and we had many dinners with dishes from their countries.

During the month of February, we had the Black History Month celebration. As always, the school choir opened the program singing the national anthem and my school song. We loved to bring awareness to the rest of the students. We also invited important government and television news reporters, like Khambrel Marshall, to talk about the historical perspective of Blacks in the USA and their accomplishments. My coworker, Mrs. B., and I were always involved in organizing these events. Unfortunately, right after retirement, she passed away. We were a great team!

At the beginning of 1990, Grandmother Aurora, who had been living with my parents, fell and hit her head. She was ninety-one years old then. She was taken to the hospital, and the doctor confirmed that she had a blood clot in her brain and needed surgery. My mother and Aunt Marta approved her surgery. We thought she was not going to survive, but to our surprise, she came through it fine. When she was discharged from the hospital, she went to live with her younger daughter, Aunt Marta, who had recently retired and was much younger than my mother. Both agreed that it was better for Mamama to move in with Marta. Anyways, they had lived together previously in Cuba and Massachusetts, so they both thought it was better for their mother.

Bobby began attending high school at a Catholic private school in Miami; it was about forty-five minutes from where we lived. He got a ride with the mother of another kid who was also attending there and lived in the area. Bob was by then teaching Bobby how to drive, so soon he could drive himself to school. He already practiced on our five-acre property. He just needed to learn the rules of the road, get the learner's permit, practice driving in traffic, and then pass the driver's test.

Chapter 10

A Summer to Remember

During the summer of 1990, at the end of a Sunday Mass at our church, the priest had a well-known community person speak to the parishioners. He was asking for volunteers to house teenagers from Spain so they could learn about the customs and family life in the USA while practicing English. These kids would be in our community for a month before returning to Spain. Bob and I raised our hands and offered our home for one of these youngsters. Several friends of ours did the same thing. We were happy to give these children the opportunity to learn English and be among us. The one we were assigned—I am going to call him Marqui—was from Barcelona, where some of my ancestors were born. He was going to spend the month of June with us.

That Friday, we went to pick up Marqui at the private high school that he and the other students were going to attend during the day for language classes. This school was down the street from the school where we were teaching. After school, it was a short walk to our school, and Marqui waited there until we finished. On weekends, we went to the beach, and sometimes we had parties at different houses.

Marqui was then a sixteen-year-old teenager with long brown hair and glasses. His clothes were fine, but his sneakers were in bad condition. Our two sons—Bobby, thirteen, and Marc, twelve—were excited to have someone new around them. We gave him Bobby's room, and our two sons slept together in Marc's room, which had its own bathroom. Marqui was a very pleasant, well-mannered, tall young man.

While at church, we were informed that another couple who had volunteered to sponsor one of the Spanish children, Geri from Cadiz, could not do so because they were still vacationing. They asked us if we could take him into our home for two of the four weeks, and we agreed to do so. Geri was also a very nice, well-mannered teenager. We purchased a foldable bed and put it in the bedroom located next to Marqui's. They shared a bathroom.

We were also asked by our friends, the Santas, if we could take their Spanish teenager the last two weeks of June. They had already made vacation plans that could not be canceled or changed, so they asked if, for the last two weeks of June, we could keep the teenager who was assigned to them. So, right after Geri went to live with his sponsors, we welcomed Eddy into our home. He was also a very well-mannered young man from Oviedo.

We agreed to help these youngsters and to give them the opportunity to learn about our culture. We were moved by our own experiences when we brought these young men into our home. The only way Eddy and Geri would have been allowed to come to the US was if we agreed to host them for the two weeks that their sponsors were away vacationing. We had enough space to accommodate them and gladly did so.

One Saturday, I was taking our sons to the barbershop for haircuts, and Marqui and Geri agreed to accompany us. I asked Marqui if he wanted to have his hair cut. He said no, but I insisted, so he then said yes. What a difference the haircut made! He looked very handsome. Then we went to a shoe store, and I offered to buy him a new pair of sneakers. He told me I did not have to buy him anything, that he had the money to purchase them. I insisted, and he finally agreed. We got him a new pair of sneakers!

A week later, while Marqui was talking with his mother, who had called him from Spain, he told me that his mother wanted to speak to me. She told me that she was very happy that he had cut his hair and gotten new sneakers. She had been trying for months to force him to do both of those things, but without any success.

His mother then began to tell me the reason why he would not do it. In October of the year before, they were involved in a car accident in which his father, a doctor, died. The last gift his father gave him were the sneakers he was still wearing. He had not cut his hair since his father died. She was very thankful to me for accomplishing this. I was glad she was happy with what I did, and Marqui was too.

Pictured below are, from right to left, Marqui; my husband, Bob; Geri; our sons, Marc and Bobby. In front of them, our Great Dane.

One day, Bob was busy cutting the five acres of lawn. Marqui and Eddy offered to help him. Bob showed them how to run the tractor. They were happy to learn!

As soon as Eddy moved in, we went to visit his two sisters, Lucy and Mary, who were staying with a young couple at the Homestead Air Force Base. We took them out for dinner, and they cried and told us that they were very uncomfortable where they were staying. They did not want to be there! We could not ignore their pleas when we had an empty master bedroom for them to use.

That evening, when we returned the girls to their sponsors, Bob and I spoke with this young couple. We explained that we had an empty guest room in which the girls could stay. Presently, they were sleeping together in a double bed in small back room next to the kitchen. This couple agreed to let them stay with us instead. This young couple told us that when they learned another host family was needed, they agreed to do it even though they did not have a comfortable place. They wanted to provide an opportunity for the foreign students to learn about our country. These young sisters were thrilled to be at our home and have a bedroom with their own bathroom, in the same house where their brother was staying. They felt much better staying with us.

Eddy's parents had won a raffle sponsored by the organizers of this mission. It was a weekend at the Fontainebleau Hotel in Miami Beach, plus airfare for two. They came with their two younger children and invited all of us for dinner at this hotel. We were twelve dining together! Eddy's parents thought we had been paid to have these youngsters in our home. We clarified the fact that we were volunteers and took these youngsters in to give them an opportunity to come to the USA and learn English; we were not paid for having them in our home. They were very thankful for our actions and happy their children were with us. When dinner was over, we tried to pay the bill, but they did not allow us!

We enjoyed a day at the Santas' family pool with all these youngsters! It was the farewell party. We were going to miss having them as part of our family. Front row, from left to right: Geri, Marqui, and Eddy. Second row: our son Bobby;

the Santas' sons, Eddy and Ivan. Last row: Mary, Mrs. Santa, Lucy, the Santas' cousin, Nery, and our son Marc.

We had a great time learning about their families. We learned that Eddy and his sisters' father was a lawyer; their mother, a pharmacist. Marqui's father was a doctor; his mother, a nurse. We were so glad they shared time with us. Marqui became a good friend, and years later, after graduating as a neurologist, he came to visit us. I am also in touch with Geri, who became an engineer. Eddy majored in history and is running his father's office. His sister Mary is a lawyer, and Lucy is a Spanish teacher in Italy.

Two weeks after they left, we received a call from Marqui's mother; she was in Miami, staying at a hotel. She had come to the Bascon Palmer Institute to have her eye checked; it was injured in the accident that caused her husband's death. Immediately, we invited her to stay with us, and she did. We had the pleasure of meeting her and spending some days with her. A neighbor took her to different places during the day while we were working.

We were happy we made the decision to open the doors of our home to these unforgettable youngsters. It was sweet to share experiences, learn about their lives, and meet some of their families. Marqui came and stayed with us again during a trip he took to the Caribbean. He was part of the family! We took a Mediterranean cruise in 2010, and Marqui invited us to stay at his home in Barcelona. After the cruise, we spent a week at his home. We met his wife, Martha. His mother showed us how to use the subway to go to La Rambla and visit all the city's tourist sites. The last night, they took us on a ride around the city. We fell in love with its beauty and history, the place where my great-grandmother Maria Barnet and other ancestors were born.

In 2019, Marqui and Martha came to visit us again and brought their two beautiful children. We were then living in a smaller house in Naples. He was invited to speak at a medical conference in Miami and took some time off to visit us. It was a pleasure to see them again. We were invited by Eddy to visit Oviedo and by Geri, Cadiz, but we have not been able to do it yet. I guess, at this time of our lives, it would be better if they came to see us here in Florida instead. We will always welcome them!

At the same time, we were very involved in our kids' school Parent Teacher Association (PTA). Bob became the president, and I, the treasurer. With the help of the two main big-brand stores in the area, we organized a fashion show using students and parents as models. We were able to raise $6,000, which helped fund many of the PTA's projects. At the end of the 1991–92 school year, we each received a plaque from the Sacred Heart School Parent Teacher Association for our dedication and excellent work. We really appreciated it.

During this same school year, I was selected Teacher of the Year and was recognized by the then school super-intendent, Roger Cuevas. I received a plaque from the Dade County School System and a certificate from Dade County's Adult and Community Education. The school principal also presented me with a plaque. I was very thankful for our teachers' support, but deep down I felt that I was just doing my job.

During the winter of 1990, we decided to use our time-share in Canada. We wanted the kids to experience a snowy winter and to learn how to ski. The resort available to us was Magog in the Canadian province of Quebec. We flew there and rented a car to drive into the mountains. It was the first time the kids saw snow! Bob was born in Geneva, New York, so he was used to that type of weather, and he already knew how to ski. For him, as with riding a bike, it was something that you never forget. For me, I got to practice my French, but no skiing.

As soon as the kids saw that it was snowing, they went outside to experience it. I even made a video of that moment and watched how Bobby slipped and fell on the icy sidewalk. He was okay, and we laughed. They began throwing snowballs at each other. It was something new in their lives and a lot of fun. On Christmas Eve, we walked to church to attend Mass. It was snowing like crazy!

On Christmas Day, by the fireplace, we opened the gifts that I had brought for them. The kids expressed that it did not feel like Christmas. They were used to celebrating Christmas Eve at our home, with our family, and then going to church on Christmas Day. After opening the gifts, we went to Mount Orford, and we found an instructor to teach them how to ski while Bob enjoyed skiing on his own. I did not want to try because I was afraid to fall and break a bone. Anyways, I did not have the right clothing either. My enjoyment was in watching my boys while sipping a cup of cocoa in front of the heated resort's panoramic windows.

We wanted Bobby and Marc to see snow for the first time and learn something new in life. But since they had missed the Christmas party with our family so much, we decided our next ski trip would be during spring break in

April, instead of the December school break. This was one of the advantages of being a teacher; we shared the same time off from school as our children.

Chapter 11

HURRICANE ANDREW HIT OUR AREA!

Our vacation in 1992 was coming soon, and we decided to spend it in Cancun, Mexico, where we had a time-share. What a wonderful time we had relaxing by the beach, enjoying the sea, and sightseeing! It was a dream come true. Like everything in life, it ended too soon. We departed on Saturday, August 22. When we arrived in Miami, we heard for the first time that Hurricane Andrew was coming, but we did not think it would be a big deal. How wrong we were!

We spent Sunday preparing for the storm. We lived in a farming area, Redland, between the cities of Homestead and Miami. We had a beautiful, large home on a five-acre farm. Bob was getting the outdoors ready while I was working on the inside of the house. Our son Marc decided to take a video of the inside and outside of the house. I even told him to help his father outside, where he was needed.

When everything was over, we realized that Marc did the right thing by recording the house before the hurricane and the way it was left afterwards. We wanted to use this information with the insurance, but it was not needed because when the insurance agent saw all the damage our property had suffered, he did not want to see any film. At least he knew we had a film of the way our house was before and after the hurricane.

We were not in the evacuation area; therefore, we decided to shelter ourselves in the house. We invited a family of six to come and stay with us. They were somehow related to me through the marriage of my father's cousin. Clara; her husband, Wayne; her parents; and her two daughters, Nicole and Amanda, who were our sons' classmates at school, arrived with their poodle at around 9:00 p.m. We were all a little apprehensive, but we went to sleep at 11:30 p.m.

After a couple of hours in bed, the howling winds awoke everyone. Clara, Wayne, Bob, and I gathered in the family room. Clara's parents and the kids were still in their bedrooms. This was really a big house with seven bedrooms and five and a half bathrooms. One of those bedrooms we used as an office and another as a music room. Clara's parents were staying in Marc's bedroom while he slept in Bobby's room. Their two daughters were staying in a room next to the boys' room. Clara and Wayne were staying in the guest room next to our master bedroom.

As the winds gained strength, from the family room, we saw the pool cage collapse and fall into the pool. Andrew's ominous power began to make us feel helpless. Soon, the front double doors began to rattle. That reminded me of a hurricane I went through as a child in Cuba at my grandparents' house; then, several men braced themselves against the door so it would not open. The sound was the same!

I told Bob that we needed to hold those doors so they would not blow open. We ran into the living room, and the four of us tried to decide how best to secure the doors. While doing so, all of a sudden, those doors burst open, and the wind tossed us like toothpicks across the room, against the wall with the fireplace. It seemed as if the devil had entered the house! Wind, rain, and debris pelted us and wreaked havoc.

We screamed as though it were the end of the world. We crawled out of the living room since we did not want to be hurt by the things that were flying around. We could hear glass breaking and the banging of debris hitting the interior walls; the whistling wind did its best to punish our home. The kids were shouting, but we hollered back and told them to stay in their rooms.

As soon as we made it into the hall, Bob and Wayne fought the wind to close the pocket door to the bedrooms' main hall, while Clara and I dragged over a chest of drawers from Marc's bedroom and shoved it against the pocket door so it would not open. Thank God for the tiled floor, which facilitated the moving of the heavy piece of furniture. We filled the gap at the bottom of the door with towels from the linen closet, which was right next to it. We rushed the kids and Clara's parents into the music room. It was the only windowless, safe room located in the middle of the house. Nine of us piled into that room—Grandpa, Grandma, four kids, three adults, and a poodle. Our Great Dane was in our master bedroom. Meanwhile, Bob was still trying his best to hold the chest of drawers against the pocket door until the wind shifted; he then joined us in the music safe room.

The portable radio we were listening to supplied the voice of meteorologist Bryan Norcross announcing that the center of the storm was passing between Cutler Ridge and Homestead. We could not believe it! It was coming to our area. What luck! It began roaring right down our throats. We would find out later that this was a category 5 hurricane with peak sustained winds of 165 miles per hour. That makes Hurricane Andrew only the third Saffir-Simpson category 5 hurricane to impact the United States since 1900. The eye did not pass over us, but we sustained the fury of the north eyewall of the storm. There was a large concentration of microbursts or tornados in the northern eyewall. Initially, the fierce winds came from the north... and blew in the front doors.

Later, at some point, the winds shifted and came from the south. When the winds shifted and came from the south, their strength pushed open the sliders of the family room and slammed shut the front double doors the northern winds had blasted open. The southern winds of that devilish Andrew were trapped in that part of the house until they pushed through the wall in the half bath, roared into the garage, threw the attic access panel aside, and sent a sheet of sheathing flying as they escaped the house through the roof of the garage.

We were all praying as loud as we could. The kids began having stomachaches. We were all terrified and afraid! The noise was horrendous; we could hear the roof tiles flying off the roof and debris smashing against the walls, glass shattering, and the whistling of the wind percolating over what was left of the plumbing stacks on the roof. During that awful time, a horrible sound of something crashing on the roof made us question if we were going to make it. We all screamed, looked at each other, and prayed louder. It sounded as if something broke through the roof and ceiling and landed in the master bedroom where our dog was.

The kids began crying for our Great Dane. We knew the hurricane was now in the master bedroom where we had sequestered our dear dog. When the noise decreased some, Bob and I crawled through the hall to our master bedroom. Its sliding-glass door was gone, and the wind was still blowing ferociously through the room. We forced our way in there as the wind whipped through the opening that used to be sliding doors. We called our Great Dane's name, and I heard his whimpering coming from the master closet. The beam of our flashlight found the anxious eyes of our frightened dog hiding under the fallen mirrored closet doors. He was okay! I called his name, and he came to me. We crawled back out of the room, led him down the hall into the safe music room, and pushed him into it. It was one of the happiest moments for all of us during this horrendous time.

We never experienced the calm of the eye of the storm. As time passed, the winds began to diminish, water began seeping through some of the rooms' ceilings, and the dim light of dawn filtered through the holes in the roof. We walked outside and saw an unfamiliar world. We had been blown to another planet! Destruction surrounded us! The Earth seemed truly flat, not round. All the beautiful landscaping that had surrounded the home was gone. It looked as though an atomic bomb had been dropped on us.

Our horses, Sorel and Osceola, were behind the next-door neighbors' house, and their cows were on our land. The house of the farm to the other side of us was destroyed. The family living there was able to survive by moving into the back garage during the hurricane, which was located at the back end of their five acres. We could not imagine how they were able to survive that treacherous trek to safety, without injury, in the middle of all that mayhem.

Two of our vehicles were in the garage, but our van and our friends' minivan were no match for Andrew's fury. We had left them parked in the driveway, side by side, in front of the doors of the two-car garage. Incredibly, now they were positioned perfectly side by side, but turned 180 degrees and relocated to the grass alongside the garage! They suffered some damage but were still drivable. The cars inside the garage did not suffer any damage other than being hit by the ceiling's drywall as it fell.

We found a forty-foot metal beam lying against the left side of the house. This beam from our neighbors' pool had caused the major damage to the roof of our house; its crash was the one that sounded like a bomb when it hit our master bedroom. Another beam from somewhere else had apparently flown over the house's roof, spinning like a helicopter blade, and digging into the roof in four different directions. We found it lying against a wall behind the house. Those two beams were the cause of almost all of the roof damage. Our house had 6,090 square feet!

Our horse Sorel had a cut on her leg. We were lucky that a volunteer veterinarian came and stitched it up. Other horses kept running to our farm from the surrounding area. Osceola began going after them, and his mother followed him. One day, I saw some people with a huge horse trailer corralling all the horses. When I saw them attempting to load ours, I ran and told them that those were ours. They let them go, and I coaxed Sorel and Osceola back onto our farm.

The damage to the entire house was unbelievable. The ceilings began to drop in some of the rooms, including Marc's room bathroom, our master bedroom, the living and family rooms, and the garage. We definitely needed a new roof and ceilings!

The insurance people came and told us that our house was a total loss. A county inspector who was going around the hurricane-devastated areas came into our home, and after looking at the house, he declared it unfit for habitation. We had to move out!

That same day, our friend Dr. S. and his family came over with the hope that ours was fine, but he was surprised to see all the damage our home had sustained. Their home was a total loss, and they had to move out too. His older son attended the Montessori School with our kids. His wife had come to our school to learn American customs and English idioms. She already had a teaching degree from India. Today, we are still very close to them, and we feel as if they are a part of our family.

When my sister Julita and Milton got divorced, Julita kept the house while Milton retained a townhouse they owned plus the dental lab. At the time of the hurricane, Milton had already divorced the woman he left Julita for, and the townhouse was empty. We rented it from him and moved into it with our Great Dane. There was no space for the dog to run around and do his business. The townhouse was just a few blocks from my mother and sisters, but far from our farm and work. We were so worried that the dog would jump the fence and run away or bite someone.

The schools were closed for two weeks after the hurricane. Then, we had to go back to our jobs when our center reopened. Our school suffered some minor damage, but we did not have electricity. The school principal obtained generators from the army and reopened the school. The area around our school sustained heavy hurricane damage, so we did not have many students when we reopened. It would take some time to get back to a full schedule of classes and attendance. My classroom already smelled like mildew.

When we returned to work, we were assigned the task of visiting the emergency camps in search of our students. Tents were set up for all the people who were left homeless by the hurricane. Many of our students were living in them, and we needed to locate them and tell them to come back to school, which was much better than staying at this camp in all the heat and with a lot of inconveniences. We also helped them enroll their children in schools near to where they were staying. We were also able to provide food for them at school.

Bob had to be at work before me, so I drove myself. One morning, driving to work, a big tree trunk fell off a truck and hit my windshield. I was so lucky nothing happened to me, but my poor car. This car was saved from the hurricane because it was in the garage, and now this. At that moment, our dear Dr. S. was driving to the hospital, and he saw what happened to me; he stopped to help. He and his family were renting in Kendall too, so he had to take the same road. After he saw that I was fine, he continued his drive to the hospital, where he was busy with a full schedule of surgeries. I had to call a towing company to haul my car to a repair shop. Dr. S. and his family moved to the Orlando area the following year. We really missed them after they left.

Our kids had an 18-mile drive to Columbus High School in Miami. They were very traumatized by what they went through during the hurricane. The worst thing was that they felt nobody else cared, and when they wanted to talk about those horrible hours, nobody wished to listen. Most of the kids at their school had not experienced as much damage as we did, but Bobby and Marc felt homeless, forced out of their destroyed home. They were in shock from what they went through and unhappy about their living situation; they saw no end to it.

We could not continue living in Kendall and driving every morning down Krome Avenue to Homestead. We were also worried that our house was unattended, the horses were running around the neighborhood, and the dog needed space. Therefore, we decided to ask the insurance company to give us a trailer that we could put in front of the house and stay there. We did that and felt much better, even though we had to keep our dog chained because the fence surrounding the five acres had been destroyed for the most part. We needed to repair it right away. The bunk beds in the trailer were too small for our teenagers. One night, Marc's foot ended up hanging out of the screened window, and the mosquitos got him. We were too uncomfortable in the trailer!

One midnight while we were staying in the trailer, a car approached the entry gate with their high beams focused on our home, blinding us. We had already heard from the neighbors that people were burglarizing the homes in the area. The dog began barking, but the car would not move.

We were so scared they were thieves and ready to hurt us. Bob jumped out of the trailer with his rifle in hand and holding Dane's leash; he yelled at them to leave. The Great Dane was ready to attack. Under those circumstances, they decided to leave. It was a tense moment!

After this scary situation, we decided to move the boys into the house's family room where they could be more comfortable. The dog stayed with them while Bob and I stayed in the trailer a little longer.

Every time we had a contractor over to give us an estimate, the first thing they wanted to know was how much the insurance paid us. We were not willing to tell them! After seeing a few men, we decided to fix our home without any outside contractors. We obtained a home-owner's permit from the county, and we were able to hire licensed subcontractors to fix our home. Priority number one was to replace the fence so we could corral the horses and the dog could run freely. Then, the roof, etc.

We went to work every morning, worried about our animals and home. One day, when we came back from work, our horses were gone. A neighbor told me that those people who had taken the other horses returned for the remaining horses in the area. According to our neighbor, the horses were taken to a huge holding pen in Miami. We went there to see if they had ours, but we did not see them. This neighbor had very expensive horses—Arabians and Appaloosas—and he was upset that they were all stolen. He hired a detective and found them on a farm in Ocala. He informed us that our horses were there too and gave us the information for us to follow up.

We called that number and talked to the lady who answered. She said that she had been helping us by feeding our horses. If we wanted them back, we had to come and get them right away and pay her for the cost of the hay. How could we bring them back when our fence was down, and we could not find someone to fix it right away? We kept trying to repair the fence, with no success. Several weeks later, the woman called and offered to release our two pintos for only $500. After thinking about it a lot, and since we were overwhelmed with all the problems we were dealing with, we decided to let the horses go. Deep inside, we feel those people took advantage of our weakness at that time. They stole our horses!

We were able to find subcontractors to do the interior work on the home while we were there since all our personal items were still there too. It took months to finally finish the house: new fence and roof installed, almost all the ceilings and some of the walls replaced, entire kitchen redone, interior and exterior of house painted, and the pool, its jacuzzi, and cage repaired. Months of hard work, but the house was finally completed. By the way, we gave a $5,000 down payment to a guy who came with a very impressive portfolio of all the work he had done repairing pools and jacuzzi. He came to work one day and never came back. Our friends, who had come to stay with us during the hurricane, gave $50,000 to a contractor to fix their home and never saw him again. So many thieves taking advantage of people's suffering!

We heard so many stories from our neighbors about what they all went through dealing with contractors who promised to have the work done right away, asked for enormous deposits, then breached their contracts or took extraordinarily long times to complete the work. I understand how difficult it was for us to find people to do the job we needed to have done on our farm. Besides, we needed to work, and the kids had to go to school. It was a very difficult year, but we always say that, thank God, we got through it and are well. Some lost their lives; many lost their homes and livelihoods due to this hurricane. There were a lot of migrants who stayed in a trailer park during the storm; they were all gone after it. Entire families were never found!

Back at school, even though we had an air-conditioning unit, my classroom still had a mildewy smell that was really making me sick! After a few weeks, I developed bad bronchitis, which eventually turned into pneumonia. I had to stay home for a week to get well. Thank God I was able to treat it with antibiotics and recover quickly. Our school was completely functional six months later, thanks to our principal.

Fortunately, we all made it through those horrifying moments, alive and thankful that the Lord heard our prayers when this more than category 5 hurricane hit our area. This was a very traumatic night for all of us which will remain forever unforgettable.

After the house was finally finished, Bob planted about 450 trees, and the farm looked great. Most of the trees were different types of mangoes, so we could have them year-round. He also planted other fruit trees for our enjoyment. The house was beautiful, and we were able to enjoy our life there once again. My brother-in-law Roly loved to come over with my sister Marita to enjoy the produce and the land. Unfortunately, he recently passed away.

One afternoon when we came home from work, a little puppy, which appeared to be a mix of chihuahua and some other breed, was at our front gate. He had ugly, crooked buckteeth and a broken jaw. Poor doggy, he really needed medical attention. The kids were excited about it. We let him inside the house so we could take care of him. We were afraid the Great Dane was not going to like him. We called the veterinarian, and he told us to bring it in right away. The poor puppy had surgery to fix his jaw, and even though we paid for the surgery, we did not need another dog. We thought about giving it to someone who was going to take good care of him. He was not a good-looking dog, but a sweet one.

After a while, he was happy because he was on the mend. We took him outside to meet the Great Dane, and the big one just sniffed him. The little one had a defensive attitude but continued walking while the huge Dane kept sniffing him. It went okay, and they got along well. The problem was that when the puppy was inside the house, the Great Dane got upset and barked like crazy. The little one was an indoor dog, but the big one was the owner of the farm.

A young couple came to the farm because they heard we were giving away a small dog. As soon as they saw his face and the buckteeth, they did not want him. Well, at this point we just kept him. The two dogs got along nicely. Daily, the little one followed the Dane as they walked the perimeter of the farm. We all pampered that little guy with so much love that he lived to be eighteen years old!

Many of the members of the Homestead Civitan Club moved away, and only a few of us were left to keep it going. I became the president. Some members wanted the club to fold, but I promised them I was going to rebuild it; therefore, we kept recruiting members, and the club became strong again. We were even able to recruit some businesses as corporate members! Our chapter became a Golden Circle Club when its membership topped thirty. We did a lot of good work in the community and were involved in building Junior Civitan Clubs. Unfortunately, the Greater South Dade Civitan Club we built in 1988 folded because most of its members, including its president, moved away after Hurricane Andrew.

Our school principal, Mr. T., called me to his office and asked me to prepare a nice Columbus Day celebration. I went home and began thinking about what we could do. I watched a movie about Christopher Columbus and decided to write a short play so the students could learn the history that way. The next day, I told Mr. T. my idea, and he agreed to it. He asked me to cast the teachers as the actors; the school was renting the costumes for the play. He called a teachers' meeting, and I shared the idea with them. To my surprise, some of the teachers were willing to act. I was Queen Isabela! Mr. Terry U. was King Ferdinando. Here are some pictures of this memorable event.

Chapter 12

IT SEEMED LIFE WAS GETTING BACK TO NORMAL

In 1993, we began the year with a wedding; Bob's brother Mike married Wendy. We all went to Sarasota, where their wedding took place. During the August vacation, we decided to visit all our relatives who live in New York and New Jersey.

We flew to New York City so the kids could see the beauty of it. We visited different museums, the Empire State Building, Central Park, the World Trade Center, the Statue of Liberty, and St. Patrick's Cathedral. We went to Ellis Island where the names of all the immigrants who came through that port were listed. Bob found his grandfather's name, Christian Kircher, listed

there. He came from Germany in 1907 when he was only eighteen years old.

We also went to visit all our families who lived up north. Bob got together with some of his mother's relatives. First, we met his first cousin, Mark, his wife, and all his children. We took the subway with them and went around New York City. He invited us to a dinner at their home, where Bob also saw his mom's only brother, Uncle Bill McCarthy. From there, we went to New Jersey to see Aunt Irma and her family. We continued driving north, all the way to where Bob is from, Geneva, New York. There, we visited his best friend, David, and his brother, Ricky, and his family. It was another great family trip and a learning experience for the kids.

Then, it was back to reality, but we were all recharged after a wonderful trip. While the kids were growing up, we always planned trips for the spring, summer, and winter school breaks. That is one of the advantages of being a teacher—spending vacations with your children. Besides that, a good pension after retirement. Teaching is a great profession if you concentrate on its positive aspects.

I understand that sometimes it can be hard to deal with the students, but there are problems in any job. The important thing is to enjoy what you do!

Regarding our cousins, we were happy that Tatoño was able to leave Cuba with his wife, Idoris, to visit his parents who were already here. They decided to stay! Unfortunately, his mother passed away that year. Their daughters, with their families, joined them—Neyda in 1995 and Liliana in 1996.

It was during that time that the adult basic-education program was going through a review, and all the adult centers were asked to write a report about it. That morning, when I came to work, the school principal called me to his office and told me about what the school department needed from all the adult centers in Miami-Dade County. Since I was the teacher who had been in the program the longest, he asked if I could write this report. From the beginning of my teaching career, I had kept a record of all my students' entry and exit scores, all the informational documents of this program, and any letters I had received from the school department, so I agreed to do it.

It took me a few weeks to gather the information and write a report regarding every aspect of this program, which involved three basic subjects: English, language, and mathematics. I also wrote about how beneficial the life skills of this program were the students. When I finished the report, I took it to the principal, and he was glad I had finished it on time. At this time, I already had my certification in administration and supervision K–12, plus adult and vocational education.

The special degree I obtained in school administration and supervision gave me the opportunity to raise my employment level and receive a better salary. I did not have any intention of becoming assistant principal since that would require that I had to drive all the way to downtown Miami to work. Besides, it would also mean a lower salary. I loved my job and the fact that in ten minutes I was home. I was also working with my husband! However, if in the future an administrative position opened up nearby, then I would consider it.

A week later, when I got to work, the principal had a visitor from the school department in his office, and the school's assistant principal was there too. As I was passing by, he called me into his office and introduced me to this gentleman as the person who had written the adult basic-education's report. The man congratulated me on a great report and wanted to know if it was okay with me for the school department to share it with all the adult centers. They thought my report was the best one. Of course, I agreed to their sharing it with the rest of the centers and was thrilled that they were going to use it. I was so glad that my report was used as an example for all the other adult centers!

Our kids were doing great at Columbus High School in Miami, and even Bobby was already driving with his brother, Marc, to school. We were always worried because the traffic in Miami was, and still is, hectic. What else can you expect in a big city? Remember, Miami is the business center for all Central and South America. To speak Spanish is an asset since that is the language of the majority of your clientele. Many of Spanish-speaking people and companies have investments in Miami, and, of course, they do a lot of shopping there for their friends and families back in their native countries. Still, you have the continuous immigration of Cubans, Nicaraguans, and Venezuelans who are running away from the Communist regime that is ruling their countries.

Our son Bobby was asked if he could work a few hours at the church's rectory so he could help the priests with the many Spanish-speaking people who came there asking for help. We let him do it. Later, he also joined the Catholic Youth Organization, as did many of his friends. That summer, they were having a conference in Philadelphia. Bobby wanted to go, so we decided to send Marc too; they could stay in the same hotel room and accompanying each other.

We were very surprised when they came back, and Marc told us that he could not sleep because the priest was snoring too loud. We were astonished when we heard this. I asked them, "And why was the priest sleeping in your room?" They told us that he asked them if he could sleep in the other bed since the two of them could sleep together in the other one. We were infuriated with the news! We felt this priest should have had his own private room, not sleep in the same room with our teenager sons. We felt he took advantage of the politeness of our children and put them in a position in which they could not say NO.

Then, I began thinking that maybe I was mistrusting the priest because of the experience I had with a priest at the same age while attending a Catholic private school in Cuba. The Spanish priest always put his arm around my shoulders, rested his hand on top of one of my breasts, and grabbed it. This made me feel very uncomfortable. When I told my mom, she went to see the school principal, a Spanish nun, to inform her of the priest's conduct. The principal called me a liar and said that the priest was a saint. My mother believed me and told me to stay away from the priest since I had only a few more months before graduation.

None of this affected my faith in Catholicism, but it opened my eyes and taught me not to be so trusting. The truth is that there are evil people in any religion. Maybe we should not have let our children go away with a bunch of teenagers and priests, or stay in a hotel, but we could not live like that, mistrusting people. But how could we have known the priest would do that? Thank God our children knew how to behave.

Things were going great in our lives; we loved the students we were teaching. Bob began doing an extra hour of teaching ABE and GED in my classroom. In 1994, a few years after we had purchased a time-share in Cancun, we decided to use it in Los Angeles to go skiing at Big Bear Mountain during spring break. I also wanted to visit my friends who lived there. It was our first time in California and the first time I would see my friend Estela since she left Cuba thirty years before.

She lived in this beautiful, large home in Anaheim. She invited us to stay with her since her daughters were away at college. We stayed that night at her house; then we went up to the cabin in the mountains. She joined us over the weekend and stayed with us at this large place with a beautiful view of the mountains. She went skiing with Bob and the kids while I stayed in the cafeteria and enjoyed my cocoa. I could see them going up and down the mountain!

I also contacted our dear Cuban neighbors who lived there. Alberto had come to Miami with his family to visit us when we bought our first house in 1974. We had not seen him since then! He invited Estela and us for dinner at his home. His younger brother, Leandro, with his wife and son, joined us too. Their older brother Leon had passed away. We are all pictured below. From right to left, front row: Estela, Leandro's son, Marc, and Bobby. Back row: Leandro, his wife, Alberto, his wife, me, and Bob.

Later, we visited Leandro at his place in the mountains on the way to the ski resort. We got together with him and his mother, and they invited us for lunch. That was the first time we had buffalo burgers! It was a memorable trip, and we had a wonderful time with our childhood friends in California!

After this enjoyable spring vacation, we were all ready to get back to school. Since this was an adult center, we dressed as if we were working in an office and provided the students with a working environment; therefore, I always tried to be well dressed at school, wearing shoes with high, thin heels and pointy toes, which were the fashion then. That style of shoe causes a lot of foot problems!

One morning, while descending the exterior third-floor stairs, my right heel caught in the step's indentation. I lost my balance and fell forward, landing on the concrete second floor. This was a concrete staircase that had sixteen steps, and each step had an indentation so the water could run off easily. When this happened, I hit the right side of my face against the railing and twisted my right pinky trying to grab ahold of it. I landed on my knees and both arms to avoid hitting my face on the ground, but still my neck sustained a whiplash injury. In this fall, both of my knees suffered major injuries and also my shoulders and neck.

One of the students who saw me falling ran to the office and asked for help. Following a painful effort to get up, I managed to limp to the main office to report what had occurred. The AP insisted that it was nothing, that I could go back to my classroom duties. I told her that I was in a lot of pain. There was no effort on her part to help me, but she insisted on having me back in the classroom. At lunchtime, I went home. My knees were swollen, hurting, and my entire body was aching. I should have gone to the emergency room!

As soon as I got home, I called my doctor and told him that I needed to see him as soon as possible. I saw him the next day, and he told me that I needed to see an orthopedist for all the damage I had done to my knees and neck. I did as he suggested, and after examining me, the orthopedist ordered that I remain off my feet for two weeks. I could not teach! I had to stay home and rest. After the two-week period was over, the doctor extended it because there was still a lot of accumulated fluid in my knees. I began receiving workers' compensation since the accident happened at school.

I could barely walk, and the doctor had to extract fluid from my right knee. The X-rays showed that I had a torn meniscus that required surgical repair. I had the right-knee arthroscopic surgery to repair the meniscus and two months of physical therapy. My knee was getting a little bit better, but it was not functioning as well as it had before the accident. I was living in pain and could not stand for too long.

I went back to work two months later. Even though my knees were still giving me trouble, I continued working and tried not to be on my feet for too long. I reviewed the students' computer work by wheeling from one student to the next in my chair, which had wheels. That way, I did not have to stand for too long. Thank God I had a very supportive principal, Mr. T.

Chapter 13

OUR SONS' HIGH
SCHOOL GRADUATIONS

In the summer of 1995, our son Bobby graduated from Columbus High School; he had already accrued twenty-one college credits. He received many awards, and we were very proud of all his accomplishments.

Before his graduation, Bob took a trip with him to Salem College in Boston. He had various study interests, one being cartography, a specialty program there. When they got there, they could not see the classrooms and labs because the professors were on strike. Bobby was interested in so many fields that he was not sure at that point what he wanted to study. He then decided to attend the University of Central Florida while he was making up his mind. Anyways, he received more scholarship money for attending a university in Florida than in another state. Whatever he decided to major in, it was okay with us. He was closer to home this way and could come home during his breaks.

Bobby was very excited, but in a way, I wished he were attending a school in Miami instead. I felt he was still too young to be away from home. But Bob's mentality was different from mine. He thought that Bobby needed to go away and grow up, to learn to do things by himself.

Often, during the summer, we went on vacation for our two-week work break in August. However, this year, we used the time to get ready for Bobby's trip to school and to take him up there to start his first semester.

We did not go anywhere during this December break either. On the contrary, we were enjoying having Bobby back home and preparing for the Christmas Eve party. We had all my family there; plus, some of the kids' friends joined us. Bobby invited some of his friends from the university. They lived in Miami and wanted to see this Cuban festivity. We were glad to meet them. He still has a close friendship with them. We were about sixty people, and, of course, Santa came to town!

Cousins Liset, Guille, Javier, Lily, Milton, Marc, Bobby, and Vivian are pictured; Marie, Frankie, and Ricky came later. Bob was Santa; Liset, the elf; and Marc was receiving a gift.

Even though my claim was a workers' compensation situation, I continued teaching the adult basic-education and GED math curriculums and helping the students to achieve their goals. My right knee continued hurting; I took painkillers to be able to work. We needed the money since we were paying for Bobby's college room and board, plus many other expenses. Besides, Marc was getting ready to go to college the following year.

Bob did a great job at school, to the point that he was selected Teacher of the Year 95–96. He was recognized at a luncheon and received a plaque from the school department and a certificate of recognition from our center. We were all very proud of his accomplishments, not only at our school but also within our family. Our children are very lucky to have a father who is a hardworking parent, who always solves our cars and household problems, and who has dedicated his life totally to his family. I can say that I am very lucky that the Lord put Bob in my path. I always say that marriage is a surprise box. Thank God that ours was a good one. We were both blessed.

Grandmother Aurora was not doing well. She was almost 100 years old but deteriorating fast. She had been a woman of very strong character all her life. Everybody always sought her advice for many of their life problems. According to Bob, she was a great cook, to the point that when I cooked, Bob always compared my food to hers... and it was to my disadvantage. Of course, she had a lot of experience cooking, and since my mother and she always did the cooking at home in Miami, I never had a chance to learn. Maybe that is my excuse, but definitely cooking is not my expertise. Unfortunately, she passed away at the beginning of 1996. We all mourned her death and will always remember our dear Mamama.

We were feeling the emptiness of our home as we anticipated Marc's going away to college. Bobby was doing very well, and we enjoyed when he came home during his breaks. I was always worried about them when they were away, but Bob always thought that it was better for them, that it was going to help them grow up and become more independent. I thought they were still too young to be so far from us.

During the spring break of 1996, we went to Orlando to see Bobby at the university. He was doing very well, and we visited Disney World. I began having chest tightness and pressure and was diagnosed with aortic stenosis that I needed to watch very closely.

Marc graduated from high school in June with twenty-four college credits, a lot of awards, and even a full scholarship if he went to a local college or university. But since several of his classmates were going to Marian College in Indianapolis, he decided to attend there; he shared a room with one of them instead. So his scholarship covered only half of his tuition, and a student loan covered the rest. We also helped with his tuition and incidentals, as we were doing with Bobby. The important thing was for Marc to be happy in the school of his selection. We were so proud of him for all his accomplishments. We surely were going to miss him too!

The injury to my knees, especially the right one, continued to be a burden. I was able to work and do my housework by taking the painkiller Vioxx. Years later, I heard that this drug could affect your heart. We hired a maid, Vicky, to clean our large home. Bob was always busy maintaining the farm. It was of great help to have Vicky give me a helping hand. I still cooked, did the laundry, kept the house organized, and did other household chores.

At this point, our huge house really felt empty without our children there. The dogs were missing them! Even though we were missing the kids, Bob and I enjoyed the privacy we had. Some nights, Bob and I went skinny-dipping in the pool! We did not have any neighbors around our five acres, so it was a very private place surrounded by trees. It was the cheapest way to entertain ourselves. We laugh now, thinking about those nights and all the fun we had in the pool.

We needed to save money to pay for all our new expenses. Having two children in college was not cheap! It was different from when I went to college. My parents did not have the means with which to support me, and I really wanted to recertify my teaching credentials in this country. I worked full time while attending college full time after work. It took a lot of discipline, dedication, and sacrifices to achieve this goal, but I did it. I always told my students that if I did it, they could too. During those years, I was concentrated on my career. No parties or going out with friends while studying. I was completely focused. My sister Julita, divorced with two children, did the same thing when she worked while obtaining her teaching degree. Thank God she had our mother who helped her with the kids.

During the summer, we flew with Marc to Indianapolis to visit Marian College, the school he wished to attend after graduation. And, of course, we had to visit the Indianapolis Motor Speedway and other nice areas while there. We liked the school, and the nuns were very nice and enthusiastic.

I got busy buying and gathering all the things he was going to need in his room while living on campus. Because those rooms were very small, Grandpa George made him a bunkbed with space on the bottom for his desk and chair. We even took that bunkbed to our Blue Ridge cabin years later and used it in one of the spare rooms.

The Christmas Eve party continued being an important family event; therefore, we always had it at our home. Every year, we assigned someone to be Santa and hand out the gifts. I made sure I began shopping around August since usually we were dealing with sixty or more gifts to give away. This was a time to get all the sisters and their families together and invite several close friends to join us. It was always a huge event for us. What a great time we always had!

We were lucky that most of the time the weather was so nice that we placed all the tables on the large porch, but if it was cold, then we needed to accommodate everybody in the family room, which was kind of crowded. Here is a picture of a group of the cousins and one of our family nucleus at our Christmas Eve party.

My sister Julita, since she was also a teacher and her kids were grown, enjoyed several vacations with us. One of them was the 1997 spring break that we went to Colorado. She bought a skiing suit and decided to learn to ski. In my case, I could not even try because of my knee injuries. Julita took lessons before she began trying by herself. Of course, Bob knew how to ski since as a kid he had lived in Upstate New York. We went to Aspen, Beaver Creek, Copper Mountain, and Vail ski resorts.

The main purpose of this trip was a second opinion on my right-knee injury. The doctor I consulted was very famous, and his clinic was in Vail. He told me that the only solution to my problem was knee-replacement surgery. While we were seeing the doctor at this hospital, Julita injured her thumb while getting off the chairlift at the resort. She was taken to the emergency room, and thank God it was just a dislocation. Her hand was immobilized, so she could not ski anymore during this trip. We were at the same hospital at the same time!

In July, Bob and I went to the Civitan International Convention at Opryland in Nashville, Tennessee. It was a great convention, and we stayed at this beautiful hotel. We visited several museums and had a wonderful time sightseeing.

· In 1997, I was selected Woman of the Year by the Homestead American Cancer Society and was recognized at a nice luncheon at the Redland Golf and Country Club. My mother, two of my sisters, and some of my coworkers attended this important life recognition. I was also given a beautiful bouquet of red roses and a silver-plated award. It was a very moving moment for me.

In August, we decided to spend a week at our time-share in Cancun, Mexico. Of course, Bobby and Marc joined us on this trip. We all needed a break from our schools! It was a two-bedroom, two-bath villa right on the beach. First thing in the morning, after breakfast, we enjoyed the beach. We also visited many of their tourist sites. We went swimming at Xcaret, the subterranean river, and had a wonderful time there. Our teenage sons had fun.

Let me give you a little bit of history. At the beginning of the Cuban revolution, Fidel Castro declared himself to be a Communist. Even though Cuba, by then, had an atheistic government, you were still allowed to worship according to your own religious beliefs. But things changed fast, and in 1969, Castro banned religious celebrations. Unfortunately, you were marked if you went to any church; therefore, people turned to cults like Santeria, voodoo, and spiritism, among others. Most of the people in Cuba were Catholics, but Castro was trying to impose atheism on its people. You were seen as an antirevolutionary for attending church!

It was an intolerable situation. People were jumping on rafts to try to make it to the United States. By then, I was sent to the forced-labor camps so my family could leave the country. Things were getting worse in Cuba. A lot of persecution and condemnation was suffered by those who disagreed with the revolution. Finally, after the visit to Cuba by Pope John Paul in 1998, Fidel Castro agreed to let religious groups celebrate their religious holidays again because he had promised the pope. It had been thirty years since the people were allowed to celebrate Hanukkah, Christmas, and other religious holidays! Still, the government kept an eye on those attending these services at different denominational churches, but at least they were allowed to practice their religions. We were already in the USA.

Chapter 14

LIFE CAN BECOME COMPLICATED

It was a nice New Year's Eve party over at my sister Margarita's as we got ready to usher in New Year 1998. The entire family and many friends came to the celebration. We were having a lot of fun!

After midnight, Aunt Marta left with Grandmother Aurora, followed by my parents. Marta lived far from the party, and our parents lived just half a block away. By 2:00 a.m., we received a call from my mother telling us that my father was not feeling well; he had a lot of chest tightness, and Mima did not know what to do.

Julita rushed over there, and when she saw how he looked, she called the 911. Then she called Margarita's house and told us that our father was being taken to the nearby hospital. Margarita told everybody to please leave because we had to go to the hospital since Pipo was being taken to the ER with chest pains. All our friends left the party, and we told our sons to drive home since we were going directly to the hospital to find out what was happening.

A few hours later, a doctor at the hospital told us that our father had a heart attack; they were running more tests, so he was being admitted for observation. The next day, he had a catheterization, which showed he had aortic stenosis plus blockage in two arteries. The surgeon came and told us that our father needed open-heart surgery to replace the aortic valve and two bypasses to circumvent the blockages.

Pipo was a heavy smoker for years; plus, he loved to have his daily drink. He stopped all of this when the doctor told him that his life depended on his quitting. He was suffering from high blood pressure and diabetes then. He did much better after quitting, but the damage to his arteries had already been done. Besides that, he remembered that he had rheumatic fever as a young man, and that caused the aortic valve stenosis. His lungs filled with fluid while he was in the hospital.

A week later, when we got to the hospital, we were told that Pipo had given his consent for the open-heart surgery the following day. We looked at his X-rays, and they still showed his lungs full of fluid. We told him that we thought his lungs were not ready for such a long surgery. He affirmed that he had already given his word to the doctor, and he wished to go ahead with the surgery. On January 7, his surgery took place. He suffered some complications, which caused the surgery to take longer and more damage to his lungs.

In June of the same year, when I went to work one morning, I walked into the mail room to get my classroom's key and tripped over some cables that were on the floor in front of the teachers' mail cabinet. Those cables were not supposed to be there! I fell forward and hit my face on a stepladder that was left in the corner of that small room. This knocked me out, and I bled profusely from my nose. I asked to be taken to the hospital where my father was staying.

It turns out I broke my nose and sustained a concussion. I was told that I needed to take it easy for a week. Eventually, when I was able to drive, I decided to spend that time looking after my father in his hospital room. At least, I could watch him while resting, and he so was glad I was there.

This was a very difficult year for my mother and the rest of the family. We had to deal with our families and our jobs, not to mention making sure someone was at the hospital most of the time, especially when doctors came to see my father. Since my mother's command of the English language was limited, we always made sure one of us was with my parents.

Because my father had spent a long time intubated, he developed an infection, so the pulmonologist decided to do a tracheotomy. Many complications occurred while he was in the hospital, and in the end, he did not have the strength to fight anymore. We were all devastated. Pipo passed away at the end of December of the same year, 1998. I wrote and published a book, *A Diary of My Dying Father*, in 2021. In it, I recount what my father went through.

Marc came home during Christmas break from Marian University. All our kids were home, vacationing from school. They were able to attend their grandfather's service. All his grandsons brought the casket into the church where the funeral Mass was held. It was a very sad moment in all our lives.

Our son Bobby just graduated from Florida State University with a bachelor's degree in informational science. We were all so happy for him. Even my father, Pipo, before he died, told him how proud he was of his accomplishments. We went to his graduation in Tallahassee. Bob's parents, George and Louise Kircher, joined us for the graduation of their first grandson. It was a very proud moment of our lives. Bobby then decided to move to Atlanta, Georgia, where he found a job working in his area of study.

Finally, Bob decided to join Civitan International. We were able to enjoy the club's meetings and projects together. I did not have to rush and cook before going to the meetings since we had dinner there. The kids were gone, our home was empty, and we needed to do something that we both enjoyed. He got so involved in Civitan that he became the president of the Homestead chapter!

My right knee continued giving me problems even though I had a lot of therapy. It seems the meniscus repair did not solve the entire issue. I continued taking the Vioxx medication the doctor prescribed. I went to see a very well-known doctor at a different hospital. He was doing something new and less invasive, partial-knee replacements. He took X-rays, ordered an MRI, and then decided that I really needed the knee surgery. He informed us that he would not know whether to perform a partial- or a total-knee replacement until he opened me up and looked at the knee. What an uncertainty!

After I woke up from anesthesia, the doctor informed me that he did the partial-knee replacement surgery and that he was hoping it was going to be fine. Again, I began having therapy, and after two months, I still could not bend my knee. The doctor told me that I needed to be readmitted to the hospital so he could bend my leg under anesthesia.

After more months of therapy, still the right knee was not well. Besides, the left knee was still giving me a lot of problems too. I began to realize how important healthy knees were for normal mobility! Still wearing a brace, getting cortisone shots to alleviate the pain, and taking ibuprofen for the swelling, I had to cope with this situation. When we went shopping, I even had to use an electric shopping cart!

Teaching became a difficult task. I talked to the principal, and he told me that he was not going to let me go back into the classroom. He gave me a position as a "teacher on special assignment." A small room near to the learning lab was prepared for me. It had a desk, a chair, one cabinet, and a printer. I brought a barstool from home so I could sit while copying documents.

At this time, our school was starting a new program in which our principal was responsible for proving teachers for the nearby Federal Job Corps. In my new position, I worked with the teachers' curriculum and guided them in the preparation of their students' individualized instruction plans. Many teachers do not know how to deal with this type of instruction. I prepared lessons to go along with their curriculums and made copies of their assignments for them. It was something that kept me busy the entire day, but I did not have to be on my feet. Most of the teachers were glad that I was giving them a helping hand with their lesson planning. I also trained the new teachers in how to deal with open-entry and open-exit individualized instruction and multilevel students' curriculums.

I put into action the curriculum knowledge I had acquired while going to the university. I had my own office, apart from the rest of the staff. Teachers came to see me during their planning time, and/or I went to their classrooms. Walking was still difficult, but, thanks to our principal, Mr. T., I was able to rest my legs since I did not have to stand for long periods of time. Besides, I really enjoyed the job I was doing.

I was still suffering with pain from the horrible fall I had on the school stairs. I was going through therapy to improve the damage that the fall had caused to my knees, but without any results. It was very frustrating to see I was not making any progress in my recuperation. The doctor insisted I give it more time to heal and feel better. That was what I did; plus, I continued taking Vioxx for the pain.

At this point, I accepted a position on the board of directors of Civitan International as its Tropical District governor. Now, both Bob and I were very involved, not only at the club level, but at the district too. We chartered several Junior Civitan Clubs in Miami, and I formed the Latin American Civitan Club, which became the Tropical Miami Civitan Club later in the year. My mother, sisters Mirtica and Julita, plus our goddaughter, Vivian, with her then husband and mother-in-law, joined too. We loved that we were paying forward all the blessings we had received. Volunteering was not optional; it was a good citizen's duty. Our mother was so proud to be a Civitan that she always wore the pin we gave her when she became a member. Vivian became the club's secretary.

During the summer of 1999, we went to Toronto, Canada, to see our first cousin Alberto and his wife Aidita; they were visiting from Cuba and staying with their daughter Yanet, her husband, Oviel, and their two children, Jhoan and Andy. It had been almost thirty years since I had seen them! He was like a brother to me. It was a very emotional moment when we all embraced. He always wanted so badly to be able to come and live in freedom, but it was not possible because his youngest daughter, Mariela, was still back in Cuba. He promised he would return to Canada as soon as he knew she was going to follow them. We had a nice time visiting with them as we took them around town.

The 1999–2000 new school year began, and I continued working in the same position I had been assigned, teacher on special assignment and curriculum assistant. I was still receiving regular knee treatments, but still my knees were not doing well. I had to wear a knee support on the right one so I could do my job. The teachers were happy that I was able to help them with their lessons, tests, and paperwork.

In November 1999, Bob was diagnosed with prostate cancer. This was devastating news for us. Thank God the doctor informed us that the cancer was enclosed in the capsule of the prostate gland and that it had not spread. Bob had to decide what type of treatment was more suitable for him because of his age, forty-nine. He was offered radiation coupled with radioactive seeds or radical prostatectomy, which were the gold-standard surgical procedures during those years. We were so worried about what would happen if he made the wrong decision. He had time to think about it and decide over the coming months.

We always went up to Lake Placid in Florida to celebrate Thanksgiving with Bob's family. Bob discussed his situation with his family. His father had prostate cancer in his seventies and opted for the hormone treatment because of his age. It never caused him any problems, and he died at the age of ninety-two from other health issues.

In December, as usual, our entire family got together to celebrate these special occasions: Christmas Eve party at our home, Christmas day at Mirtica and Jack's home, and New Year's Eve party at Margarita and Frank's home. We always had a great time celebrating these special days.

After Bobby graduated from college, he got a job at a well-known company in Atlanta and in the field he had studied. We picked him up in Tallahassee, where he had been going to school and helped him move. We dropped Bobby at his new place in midtown and continued up north to the mountains to visit Bob's sister, who had a house on a lake in Blairsville, Georgia.

Bob loved that area and was thinking about getting a property there. He was entertaining the idea of moving out of Miami-Dade County after retirement because it was getting too crowded. I did not like this idea too much since all my family was in Miami, and we had always lived close to each other. But Bob was thinking that we could enjoy the winter months in our condo on Marco Island and the rest of the year in the mountains.

My sister-in-law's place was on a beautiful lake, and the house was big and spacious with wonderful views. We cruised around the lake on her boat, enjoying every minute of it. Bob made up his mind; he wanted a property there, close to his sister. We visited a new gated community up on a mountain with an uninterrupted, picturesque view of the Blue Ridge Mountains. The price was reasonable, and we left the area with the thought of maybe purchasing one of these affordable cabins in the future. Years later, we bought a small cabin in this gated community. I really wanted one lakefront; therefore, later on, we had a lodge built on a lake, which I loved.

One day while we were in our lodge, I was not feeling well; I decided to go to the local clinic. The doctor informed me that not even their local hospital had a defibrillator, and they had to send sick patients by helicopter to a hospital some distance away from there. I could not believe it! Eventually, the clinic got a defibrillator, but still, it was very risky to move up there with my heart situation.

In the end, we decided to sell both properties in Georgia and buy a place in Naples, Florida, where we have been living since 2008. We were glad we made this decision and have been enjoying our retirement since then.

Chapter 15

TIME TO FACE REALITY

We welcomed the New Year 2000. One morning in January, the assistant principal came to tell me that I could not continue in my special position; she wanted me to immediately start teaching the English as a Second Language (ESL) class. I explained to her that I was still having physical therapy and a lot of issues with my knees, that I could not stand in front of a classroom and teach for hours. She even offered me a wheelchair! I refused to do what she was telling me to do, so she told me to go home; they no longer had use for me at the school. I could not believe it!

I called a friend who was injured at work and using a lawyer. She gave me her lawyer's name, and I called him right away. He told me to follow the order the assistant principal gave me and leave work, to call the Workers' Compensation Department and let them know what happened. He set an appointment in his office for the following day. Crying, I took all my things and left the school. The teachers and staff who saw me leaving asked what happened, and I could not speak. It was a very painful moment.

The next day, I went to see the lawyer, and he issued a demand against the school system. I began receiving workers' compensation payments and continued to do so until my case was settled in May 2000. I received compensation for the damages I suffered in that awful fall and my full retirement. I still felt young and useful, but in a different way. The school staff wanted to give me a retirement party, but I told them no because I felt I was forced into leaving. Years later, I realized that it was the best thing that could have happened to me since I had to face a lot of health issues, and thank God I was at home, not dealing with a job. Sometimes, things happen for a reason.

Bob chose to have the radical prostatectomy, which took place on February 14, 2000. How ironic! He was devastated, but I kept encouraging him, sending him good vibes, and telling him that everything was going to be fine. He had the best surgeon in Miami, who did a great job sparing the surrounding nerves. Bob did very well, and his surgery was a success. We were aware that our passionate sex life was not going to be the same as before, but the important thing was that he was alive and doing well, thank God.

During this time, I was once again diagnosed with aortic stenosis, which we began to watch closely. The cardiologist was very worried because of the narrowing of the aortic valve was growing more severe. He told me to be careful; if it continued getting worse, I was going to need an open-heart surgery similar to my father's to replace the aortic valve. I was much younger than my father was when he was diagnosed though. The doctor told me to try to stay away from worries and life pressures, something that I thought was impossible.

My poor mother was constantly praying for the health and welfare of her daughters. I feel her prayers were heard. She also worried about her grandchildren and made sure all eleven of them—four girls and seven boys—were fine. She joined the charismatic group at church and was very involved in a prayer group. I am sure, at this moment, my mother is watching us from heaven and still praying for us.

During the summer, we went to Indianapolis for our son Marc's graduation from Marian University. We were so proud of all his accomplishments. He graduated with two majors—musical theater and vocal performance—and his dream was to become a singer. He was able to find an acting job at the Actors' Playhouse at the Miracle Theater in Miami. We were always there, enjoying their musical plays and very proud of his acting. He was also made the house manager at the theater. Marc rented an apartment, with a

friend who was also an actress, near the theater in Coral Gables. He was in the apartment for more than a year, but when his friend moved to another country, Marc moved back in with us. Even though the theater was a bit far from where we lived, he did not care. We welcomed him back with open arms…his cat, Mary, too.

My right knee was getting worse, but Bob was doing very well after his cancer surgery, thank God. We were happy about that. Volunteering for Civitan gave me the chance to work at home doing all the paperwork, organizing activities, recruiting new members, forming new clubs, etc. The good thing about no longer teaching was that I had more time to be a volunteer at the Homestead Civitan Club and the Civitan Tropical District, and they really appreciated the hours I spent helping the organization as a leader. As I said before, it was our duty to serve others.

In July, we went to the Civitan International Convention in Norway, Oslo. It was our first time in Norway. We could not believe there was still daylight past midnight. In order to sleep, we had to close the heavy curtains at the hotel to keep the light from filtering into the room.

The next day, we went for a walk in the downtown area. I began getting cold, but had not brought anything to protect me from the weather. We went into a store and bought me a spring coat. It was a beautiful, long black-leather coat that was on sale for $100. Without any hesitation, I purchased it and put it on. Guess what? I never wore it again in Florida. After several years, it did not fit me anymore. Recently, I gave it to one of my grandnieces, my god-daughter Emily, since she went away to college in one of the northern states. She needed it there, and it fit her perfectly.

The day after that, we went on an excursion outside Oslo. We visited the fjords and the Viking Museum. We also went to a glass factory in which we saw a young man wearing a Florida Marlins T-shirt. I told Bob that I thought he was Cuban. I yelled in Spanish, "¿Eres cubano?" ("Are you Cuban?") He yelled back, "Yes, I am," and came to talk to us. He told me that he met a Norwegian family in Cuba, and they helped him get out of the country. When he got to Norway, he began going to school to learn the language. Then, he met this beautiful blonde girl with big blue eyes and married her. We gave him some money, and, of course, he was very happy to meet us. During the excursion, we learned about Norway's type of government, a monarchy, and enjoyed the beauty of the country.

At night, we attended the Civitan International President's Social at the Oslo City Hall, where the Nobel Prize is presented every year. That was a very special evening, and we enjoyed admiring all the huge wall paintings. It was a very memorable moment too. During the Civitan International Awards Ceremony, I received the Distinguished Governor's Award 1999–2000 from the Civitan International President, Leroy Parks, something that only a few governors receive every year. The Tropical District that I was governing received the Membership

Award for growth and retention. We had a good group of district members attending this convention. We were very proud of all our accomplishments and the recognition.

From Oslo, we traveled to Paris, France. It was our first time there too. We stayed at a hotel just one block from the Arc de Triomphe. Sunday, July 14, everybody at the hotel kept saying, "Hurry up; don't miss the Bastille Day parade!" Well, we walked half a block to the main street, which took us to the Arc de Triomphe, where the parade started. When we got there, right in front of us was French President Jacques Chirac, who was leading the parade. I videotaped this special moment in our lives. Who knew we were going to see the president of France just a few steps from us! The parade was magnificent and enjoyable. When it was over, we went to get lunch, but most businesses were closed. Finally, we found one open café where we had a ham and cheese sandwich. That was the only item on the menu on this great holiday for Parisians.

The next morning, we went on an excursion to Normandy, something that Bob wanted to do while in France. It was a very moving trip to Omaha Beach, where the American troops landed on June 6, 1944, D-Day, to fight the Nazis during World War II. We saw the town where all of this took place, even though we had already seen it in movies. When we got to the beach, we could not believe that, still, in the deep sand were some of the portable docks that brought the soldiers to the beach. We could also see some remnants of the landing crafts in the water since we were there at low tide. It was a memorable moment.

We visited the American cemetery. Just seeing all those crosses in the silence, the wind blowing our hair, gave us knots in our throats. We felt as if we were going to cry while seeing the evidence of so many young lives lost in that war, on that beach. What a sad sight!

When we left there, we went to the museum where you could see movies of the real fight, artefacts left behind, and documentation of what occurred there. The Allies successfully pushed the Nazis out of Western Europe and turned the tide of the war for good. The sacrifice they made for freedom will never be forgotten. Germany would surrender less than a year later, on May 7, 1945, ending the war in Europe. It was a memorable trip, one we have never forgotten, especially since it was our first time visiting that part of Europe, the continent where our ancestors were born.

At this point, my aortic stenosis had been worsening, and I was having a lot of chest tightness. Also, my mom was diagnosed with pulmonary fibrosis, and this was devastating news too. We could not imagine why she got this disease. She never smoked, but my father always smoked around us. Could this have caused my mother's sickness? Who knows! Whenever she was sick, someone from church brought her Communion, and friends came over to pray for her.

Bob and I continued our mission of paying forward to the community by volunteering at our local Civitan Club. We had several leadership positions at the club and district levels. We made many friends and loved to join them at all the meetings, especially all of those we met from all over the world at the Civitan International conventions. Attending functions, we have visited many states of the United States. Bob and I both received the Foundation Fellow Award in recognition of our contributions to the ideals of Civitan and our dedication to the youth through participation in the Civitan Shropshire Scholarship program. Again, I received the Distinguished Governor Award 2000–2001 from Civitan International President Eva Wilhelmsen from Norway. We loved helping the community!

My aortic stenosis was getting worse, and the cardiologist ordered a heart catheterization. After I had it done, he came to see me with a surgeon who told me that my heart's aortic valve was almost completely closed; I needed to have it replaced right away. He was the surgeon who operated on my father's aortic stenosis. Both doctors suggested I stay in the hospital and have the surgery the next day. But I told them that I had a lot of personal business to take care of before the surgery; I needed to go home and get my affairs in order.

When I got home, I began studying the options for repairing aortic stenosis. One of them was the Ross procedure, in which the aortic valve is replaced by my pulmonary valve. It would then function as my aortic valve. In turn, a valve from a human cadaver would be used to function as a pulmonary valve. This surgery was done mostly for younger people and children, people for whom the aortic valve would last longer.

I called the Cleveland Clinic in Ohio, and they informed me that there was a doctor in Hollywood, Florida, who was trained by them to do this procedure. I made an appointment to see him, and after much study and testing, I was selected as the oldest patient to have the Ross procedure done by that particular surgeon. He felt, because I was still young, I could have the valve replaced this way in lieu of a conventional mechanical or porcine valve, which were the standards at that time. I wasn't in favor of these options because the mechanical valves were metallic, and those people whom I knew who had them said their heartbeats were loud. My deceased father's valve was replaced with a porcine valve.

My father's and my aortic stenosis were both the result of the rheumatic fever we had as youngsters. I remember I was a teenager when I had it. Who knew that illness would affect my heart valves and threaten my life decades later? If the rheumatic fever had been detected right away and treated with antibiotics, neither my father nor I would have experienced these complications. Parents need to be aware of this when a child complains of swelling and pain in the joints and sore throats. I learned all of this after I was diagnosed with aortic stenosis.

On August 30, 2001, I had my first open-heart surgery at the Holy Cross Hospital in Fort Lauderdale, Florida. Bob, my mother, Aunt Marta, and two of my sisters were at the hospital during my surgery, which took five hours because of a complication. When the doctor put the heart back into the cavity, one of the main arteries kinked, and I had to have an emergency bypass. They had to stop my heart again to repair this damage. Thank God everything else went well. I felt much better a few months after my surgery. This family picture was taken before my surgery.

During this time, my sister Julita was diagnosed with breast cancer. Another blow to our mother, who suffered as she witnessed her girls going through difficult times. My sister needed immediate surgery. Hers was a very aggressive form of cancer; therefore, she had to have a double mastectomy. Her surgery went well, and it was followed by very strong chemo treatments. She did not even have enough strength to get off her couch. Thank God our mother was living with her, so she took care of my sister's needs during this difficult process. My sister lost all her hair! Still, she stayed strong. I had to drive her sometimes to her doctor because she did not have the strength to do it, and I was the only one at home since the rest of my sisters were working. Thank God none of us has suffered from this awful disease again, and let's pray it continues this way.

Julita has always been a very strong woman who, unfortunately, has faced many difficult things in her life, especially what has afflicted her for the last fifteen years—Parkinson's disease. It might be attributed to ten years of working at a tree nursery. She was a bookkeeper in the office; unfortunately, the room in which she worked also housed fertilizers, weed killers, and other toxic substances. She was breathing air full of chemicals! Years later, in 2022, she had a deep-brain stimulation surgery to stop the Parkinson's involuntary movements. It was successful, and now she is doing much better, thank God.

My mother's sickness continued to progress. Eventually, she had to stop dying her hair, but she was still the one who always made us laugh. This picture was when she turned eighty years old. Pulmonary fibrosis is another terrible sickness that steals from you not only the capacity to breathe, but the lack of oxygen to your brain can lead to dementia. She passed away in 2007. All her grandsons carried her casket into the church. Our son Marc sang a beautiful song his grandmother composed, *"Viento"* ("Wind"), and the "Ave Maria." It was a very moving funeral Mass.

Chapter 16

Closing This Part of Our Lives

This is the last chapter of this compilation of special moments in our family life before and after we arrived in the Land of the Free. I have recounted these events to best of my recollection; however, maybe some family members will remember them differently.

My intention with this book is to inform others that as refugees, our lives were not easy at the beginning, especially for my parents who came here at an older age with nothing but the clothes on their backs. It took them longer to assimilate into a new culture. Adjusting to this new country, its language, and its customs was not as easy for them as it was for their daughters. My father was able to communicate with the limited English he had learned in Cuba. My mother, however, did not have an ear for English. Even taking English for Speakers of Other Languages (ESOL) classes did not help her. She told us that when she was in high school in Cuba and took English as a second language, she could not retain it. She really suffered for not being able to communicate with others in English. At least she could converse with my husband, Bob, who knew Spanish.

My parents made sure that their grandchildren continued speaking the Spanish language. Every time my mother babysat them, she addressed them in Spanish, and the kids got used to replying in it. I am not sure about some of our third-generation family members, but most of our nieces and nephews have made sure they use Spanish at home to help their children become bilingual. My parents tried very hard to pass on our Cuban roots, values, and traditions to their grandchildren, as we did with our children.

Our home was different. Bob spoke English with me; that was the language our children heard most often, even though I usually spoke to them in Spanish. At their elementary school, most of the kids were Americans who knew only one language—English. Both of our children can communicate in Spanish, especially Bobby since his Spanish improved a lot while spending time in Mexico and Spain. He also loves to practice, speaking to me in Spanish, so that he can keep his fluency. It is an advantage to be at least bilingual! My husband, Bob, had three years of Spanish in high school, a couple of years in college, and an interest in learning more. He had the chance to practice it with his customers too. Maybe he wanted to know what my sisters and I were talking about! He laughs when I tell him this.

Talking about when we met, Bob told me he was encouraged to invite me out for a date since he already knew my father. Shortly after this discovery, he finally invited me to a lobster dinner, an offer I could not refuse. We were made for each other! We both found true love and have been married, this coming June, for forty-eight years. There are no regrets on my part, and I am sure he would say the same. We have always tried to settle any dispute before going to bed. We trust each other and try our best to show our love. We have been faithful all these years, and thank God we still love and respect each other. The best decision of my life was to marry him!

As you have read in this book, we have been through ups and downs in our lives. Who has not?! The worst times we faced involved health issues; we both are survivors of deadly diseases—cancer and cardiac disease. We thank God for the blessings we have received. It seems to me there's a good reason that we have won the battles against these diseases for the most part.

We have dedicated many hours of our lives to helping others in the communities where we have lived. Maybe that's why our lives were spared. Volunteering is an unselfish act that helps you socialize and develops your sense of kindness. You become grateful that you are still useful and thankful for being physically able to help others. It does not matter how you do it; just do it! Your life has a purpose, a meaning other than work and family. Pass this concept on to your children so they follow in your footsteps. And remember, I have always heard that volunteers live longer!

Our children grew up in two different cultures, and they assimilated the best from each, as we all have done. They love Cuban as well as American food. They feel they are Cuban Americans even though they were born in the USA and have an American father. I am glad they feel that way. They enjoyed the attention of their Cuban grandparents and great-grandmother when they spent some time with them. They also enjoyed our Cuban family's gatherings at our home and the ones over at my sisters'. They also loved their American grandparents, uncles, and aunts, and the time they spent with them.

I decided to write about our lives up to the time right after our twenty-fifth wedding anniversary and my first open-heart surgery in 2001. I had a second surgery in 2015 to repair a large aneurysm in the ascending aorta, close to the aortic valve. The aneurysm was repaired by dissecting it and sewing it back up. The aortic valve was replaced by a bovine one. Today, nine years after that surgery, the aneurysm is present again in the same location. Tests and scans have determined it to be of greater size than the previous one that required surgery. I am also having some issues with leakage in some of my other valves that need to be repaired.

This would be my third open-heart surgery. I consulted with three other surgeons, and they all just told me to continue enjoying life because this surgery's survival rate is very low. I finally found a surgeon who would attempt a third open-heart surgery using a method that ensures a lasting fix of the aneurysm and has a high survival rate.

Bob and I went to Houston, Texas, to see the heart surgeon that specializes in aneurysm repairs; he had operated on a friend of mine. He told me that I had an 80-percent chance of surviving the surgery. I am still debating if I should have this surgery. Right now, he is reviewing my tests and scan results and will let me know soon how and when he can do the surgery. My purpose at this moment is to publish this book before my surgery, if I decide to have it.

Apart from my heart issues, I had a total right-knee replacement in 2004, but still the left knee continued giving me trouble. I began a course of hyalogen injections, which brought some relief. Eventually, I had the platelet-rich plasma treatment, which really made a big difference in my left knee. The right knee does not bother me, even though I cannot bend it well.

Our families are our priorities, and we keep in close contact with them. Bob and I are constantly in touch with our brothers and sisters. I speak to my sisters almost every day, and Bob is in touch with his family regularly. I am sure our parents in heaven are glad to see their children loving and caring for each other. That was the way they raised us.

We are very proud of all our accomplishments, we are thankful for our children and families, and we thank God for all his blessings. Bob and I have been very supportive of each other, through good and bad times, and that is very important in the life of a married couple. We have been sympathetic to one another during our health issues and have enjoyed a great time together throughout the years.

My sisters and I are thankful to our parents for bringing us to the United States of America, where we found the freedom that we were denied in Cuba. It was sad to see our parents die without seeing Cuba become a free nation once again. At this moment, I feel the same way they did. I thought I was going to have the happiness of being able to go back and see a free Cuba during my lifetime. I have never been back there because of all that my family and I went through. I am afraid of being accused of something and getting sent to jail or another forced-labor camp. You never know with that system; there is always an uncertainty about what could happen to you there. It is unbelievable that Cuba has had sixty-five years of Communism even though it is only ninety miles from the United States.

By the way, we like to take cruise vacations and we have been on thirty-six of them. On one recent cruise, we went to the island of Grenada in the Caribbean Sea. On an excursion, the guide told us the history of that tiny island. In 1979, a Communist revolution installed a Socialist government in the former British colony. Four years later, during President Ronald Reagan's first term, this Marxist government took control of the island while more than 1,000 American students were studying at the medical school there. The president decided to act, citing the danger to the students in Grenada. Reagan ordered nearly 2,000 US troops onto the island, where they soon found themselves facing opposition from Grenadian armed forces, groups of Cuban militias, and so-called "engineers" who were in Grenada to complete the island's new military-civilian airport. The Grenadian government had groups of Cuban militias seeking the advice of the Communist Cuban government on how to establish the new Communist government on the island. Cuba sent troops to help the military during the invasion.

The tour guide told us that in 1983, the US, with the assistance of a coalition of six other Caribbean nations, invaded the island. The American intervention was a success because it prevented a Communist takeover. They restored a constitutional government and Capitalism to this Caribbean island nation. Grenada is part of the chain of Windward Islands, the southern group of the Lesser Antilles in the West Indies. It is an independent island state within the Commonwealth of Nations. It is one of the smallest independent countries in the western hemisphere.

Listening to this Grenadian tour guide, I wondered if Cuba, my birthplace, would ever be rid of Communism and join the democratic nations of the Western Hemisphere. It hurts me to see all the misery the Cuban people have been enduring; it has been going on for generations, and all other nations have been ignoring what is happening. When are the United States and other countries going to act and free Cuba? Maybe the people need to revolt against the Communist dictatorship. Recently, Cubans have been peacefully protesting the Communist regime and chanting, *"Hambre* (hunger), *electricidad* (electricity), and *libertad* (liberty)."* The country situation has been getting worse for them. Hopefully, it will happen soon!

Looking back, I want my family and friends to know how glad I was to take each step in my life. It has been a great learning experience in two different worlds, under two different types of governments, cultures, languages, etc. I have met beautiful people who have left an impression on me. Great friends have come and gone, but they are still in my heart. We have lived in two cultures, and our children have learned the best of both worlds. All my sisters have been supportive, and thank God we are still very close. Our parents really taught us to love each other and be there when the need arises.

Thinking about my ancestors, I am sorry for what they went through—the terrible experiences and horrible times escaping from the government's persecution, losing dear ones in their search for freedom. Then, I compare their experiences with ours and realize that we were very lucky that we did not have to endure the pain of losing someone in our running away from the government.

At this important time in our lives, Bob and I are loving all the things we do together, such as socializing with friends, going out for dinner, and singing karaoke. We met wonderful people when we moved to Naples, Florida;

they share our passion for music. We feel that socializing is important. Do what you like to do, enjoy life, and pay forward your blessings by giving a helping hand where it is needed. Therefore, we continue volunteering in the name of Civitan.

As you read in this book, my family faced many challenges when we came to the USA: a new culture, a different lifestyle, and a new language, but with courage, discipline, and a desire to succeed, we all were able to achieve the American dream in this great nation. We are praying for the best with my surgery, if it happens, and when everything is over, I will continue writing the rest of the story of our lives.

Many blessings to all and to all a goodbye. God bless the United States of America!

Bibliography

GOOGLE

Congressional Record – Senate – Letter of
    Owen Melton dated June 6, 1896 –
    Special dispatch to the press.

My Heritage

Universidad de Las Palmas de Gran Canaria
    Tesis Doctoral:

"El emigrante retornado a Canarias desde
    América," 1870-1940.

Wikipedia

Acknowledgments

A special thank-you to my husband.

He guided me and supervised what
I was writing.

He refreshed my memory of many
instances of our life together.

He was the lighthouse that guided my
ship so I could arrive at a safe port.

Thank you, honey.

Nery Barnet Kircher has been writing since an early age. The first book she published was in 1983, *Algo de Mi*, which is a collection of her poems. After retirement, she began writing her memoirs. She had to put it away many times because of painful memories. Finally, during the COVID pandemic, she published *Path to Freedom*, which became a bestseller on Amazon and appeared in Halo Publishing Company's *History of Cuba* in January 2021.

In this book, she begins by telling the story of her ancestors, their family life during different governments, and her experiences in the forced-labor camps she had to endure to be able to come to the USA. In mid-2021, she published its Spanish translation, *Camino a la Libertad*. At the end of the same year, she published *A Diary of My Dying Father*, dedicated to the family's struggles for the survival of their father.

Her talent is not limited to writing; it includes music. As a music composer, she has received multiple awards. She believes that she inherited her know-how from her talented mother, Elena Maria.

Nery is a very dedicated, civic-minded volunteer, and she has received many commendations for her community involvement. She has been an active member of Civitan International, an organization dedicated to serving the needs of communities around the world, with an emphasis on those suffering from intellectual and developmental disabilities. She feels that she needs to pay forward all the blessings she has received.

Nery loves to sing and has passed this passion on to her children and husband, Bob. One of their favorite shared activities is karaoke. She thinks that it is wonderful to enjoy a delicious dinner with friends while singing or listening to others sing. "What a nice way to socialize!" she says.

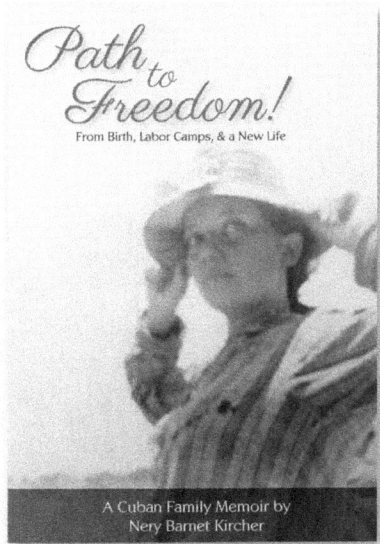

Path to Freedom!
From Birth to Labor Camps to a New Life

ISBN Paperback: 978-1-61244-935-7

This is the story about a Cuban family from their very beginnings. This story includes descriptions of their ancestors, which are part of their legacy, and it tells the struggles suffered by its author from the sixties to 1971, when she and her family arrived in the United States.

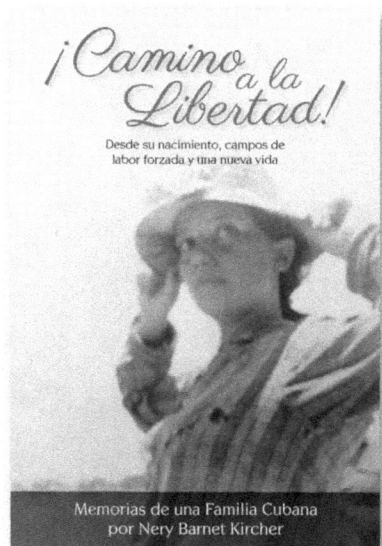

¡Camino a la Libertad!
Desde su nacimiento,
campos de labor forzada y una nueva vida

ISBN Paperback: 978-1-63765-008-0

Esta es la historia de una familia cubana desde sus comienzos. Sus anécdotas incluyen descripciones de sus antepasados, quienes son parte de su legacía.

Habla de las luchas que su autora sufrió durante los años sesenta hasta 1971, cuando ella y su familia llegaron a los Estados Unidos de América.

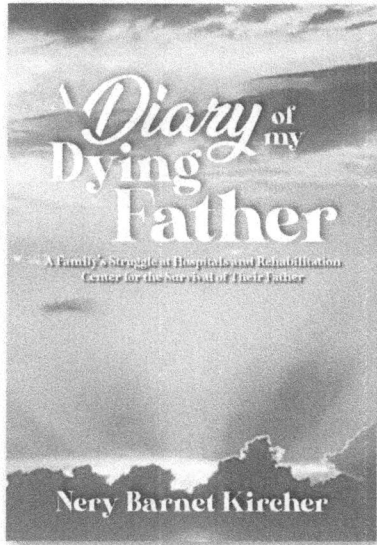

A Diary of my Dying Father
A Family's Struggle at Hospitals and Rehabilitation
Center for the Survival of Their Father

ISBN Paperback: 978-1-63765-136-0

This book, which relates to a diary kept during the year 1998, is about what this family went through after their father had a heart attack. It is an odyssey of his fight to survive the mistakes committed by the people who were dealing with his sickness while he was hospitalized and being rehabilitated. At the end, his journey was fatal.

www.ingramcontent.com/pod-product-compliance
Lightning Source LLC
Chambersburg PA
CBHW060305100426
42742CB00011B/1869